TAKING ROOT
Jewish Immigrants in America

ALSO BY MILTON MELTZER

TAKING ROOT

Jewish Immigrants in America

MILTON MELTZER

FARRAR, STRAUS AND GIROUX | NEW YORK

Library of Congress Cataloging in Publication Data
Meltzer, Milton
Taking root.
Bibliography: p. includes index.
1. Jews in the United States—Social conditions—Juvenile literature.
2. Jews—Migrations—Juvenile literature. 3 United States—Emigration and
immigration—Juvenile literature. [1. Jews in the United States—Social conditions. 2. Jews—Migrations. 3. United States—Emigration and immigra-
tion] I. Title.   E184.J5M46   1976   301.45'19'24073   76–18169
ISBN 0–374–37369–8

301.45
me 62

ACKNOWLEDGMENTS

Acknowledgment is made for permission to quote from the following
works: *The Time That Was Then*, by Harry Roskolenko, Copyright © 1971
by Harry Roskolenko, by permission of The Dial Press; *The Promised
Land*, by Mary Antin, Copyright 1912 by Houghton Mifflin Company,
Copyright 1940 by Mary Antin, by permission of Houghton Mifflin
Company; *A Lost Paradise*, by Samuel Chotzinoff, Copyright 1953, © 1955
by Samuel Chotzinoff, by permission of Alfred A. Knopf, Inc.; *Green
Worlds*, Copyright 1938 by Maurice Hindus and *A Traveler in Two
Worlds* by Maurice Hindus, Copyright 1971 by Frances McClernan
Hindus, both reprinted by permission of Doubleday & Company, Inc.;
The Ghetto, by Louis Wirth, ©1928 and 1956 by The University of
Chicago Press, by permission of the University of Chicago Press; *The
Spirit of the Ghetto*, by Hutchins Hapgood, © 1966, by permission of
Funk & Wagnalls; *Art Is My Life*, by William Zorach, © 1967, by per-
mission of Thomas Y. Crowell Company, Inc.; "Revolt of the Reefer-
Makers," by S. L. Blumenson, Copyright © 1949 by The American Jewish
Committee, and "Rutgers Square," by S. L. Blumenson, Copyright ©
1950 by The American Jewish Committee, both reprinted by permission
of *Commentary*; *The Rise of David Levinsky*, by Abraham Cahan, © 1917
and 1945, by permission of Harper & Row; *A Dreamer's Journey*, by
Morris R. Cohen, Copyright 1949 by The Free Press, by permission of
Macmillan Publishing Company, Inc.; *Shadow and Light*, by Maurice
Sterne, © 1965, by permission of Harcourt Brace Jovanovich. The songs
on pages 39, 96, 140, and 236 are from *Voices of a People* by Ruth Rubin,
Copyright © 1973, 1963 by Ruth Rubin, by permission of McGraw-Hill
Book Company.

*To Mary Richter and Benjamin Meltzer,
the young immigrants,
with love*

Contents

Foreword

I hope this is a book that can be enjoyed for itself. But the reader should know it can also be read as part 2 of *World of Our Fathers: The Jews of Eastern Europe*. In the earlier work I tried to present a panoramic view of Jewish life in Eastern Europe, that culture from which most of today's six million American Jews came. The book ends at the time of the great migration of the Jews from Eastern Europe. This book takes up where that one left off. It tells the story of innumerable families like my own. My grandfather, Samuel Richter, decided America was the place to raise his children, not Austria-Hungary. So he got up from the village of Skoryk, and left. Sounds easy, doesn't it? I never stopped, until recently, to imagine what it must have been like for a young father to make that decision. To quit the place he grew up in, to leave wife and children behind, to strike out across the unknown countries of Europe for a distant seaport, then to take steerage passage across the frightening Atlantic, and at the end of a harsh voyage, drop like some anonymous atom into the vast chaos of New York. Where would he find a place to sleep? What could he do to make a living? How would he make himself understood in a language he didn't know?

It was 1895 when Samuel Richter came to America. Didn't stay long; went back in 1897. Why? I don't know. Too lonely? Unable to earn enough to bring the others over? But two years later, after fathering three more children (including a pair of twins), he decided to try again. And the next year, 1900, my mother, Mary, followed him. She was fourteen then, the oldest of her many brothers and sisters, a capable girl, with enormous energy and will. Together she and my grandfather earned enough to bring over the rest of the family in 1903.

Millions of others did it too. Jews like them and non-Jewish immigrants, chiefly Greek Orthodox and Roman Catholic, from all the countries of Eastern and Southern Europe. My father among them. Benjamin Meltzer was eighteen when he left the village of Havrilesht in the Austro-Hungarian province of Bukovina. He reached New York in 1897. He was the oldest of five brothers and two sisters. He came first, and alone. Later one of his sisters and two of his brothers joined him. But his mother and father (my grandparents) and one sister and two brothers did not come. He never saw them again.

Mary and Ben met in New York, married, and moved to Worcester, Massachusetts, where they raised three sons. My father died at the age of fifty-seven, my mother at seventy-seven. Nobody outside their family and small circle of friends ever heard of them. But the quality of their lives, the delights and disappointments, the ambitions and fears, the labors and illusions, are here, I hope, in this story of their immigrant generation.

I wrote this story of the Eastern European Jews because they are my people and I wanted to learn about them. But what happened to them, in many respects, is like what happened to all the other immigrants, whatever their origin. There were differences, of course, and most significant ones; each ethnic group has its own historical memory, real and imagined, and whether it is our own or not, worth exploring.

TAKING ROOT
Jewish Immigrants in America

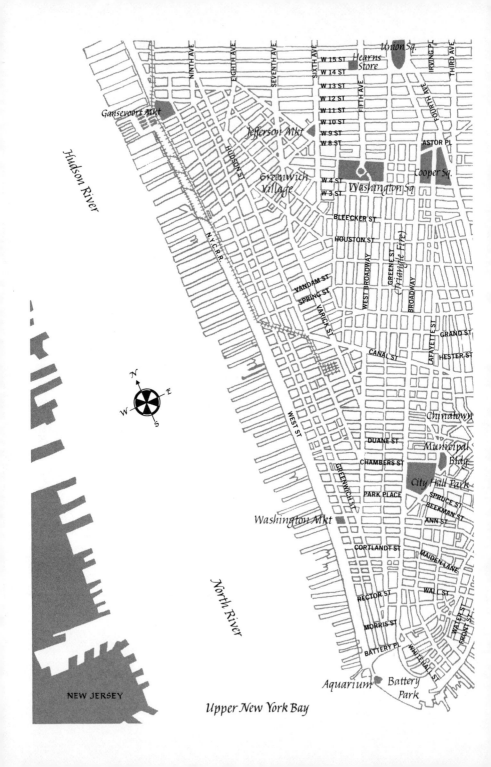

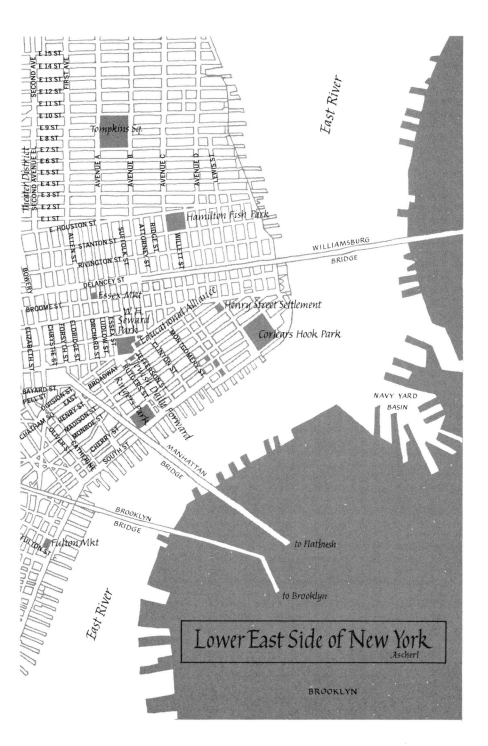

1 | Less Than a Dog

Maurice Sterne was only a little boy when he got his first practical lesson in what it meant to be a Jew in Czarist Russia.

He was walking with his mother on a street of small Jewish shops in his home town of Libau when suddenly—

A great noise of shouting men and horses' hoofs exploded behind us and without once looking back my mother ran with me into the shelter of a nearby doorway. A small company of Cossacks charged around a corner and into the narrow street where they laughed and cursed and swung their nagaikas, *those infamous long whips. The crowd scattered in panic beneath their feet, and though that day no one was caught under the horses, the whips lashed out with agonizing accuracy. I have never forgotten the dreadful sound of that street, when the derisive Cossack blare mingled with the sharp, thin scream of their victims' terror. And my soul has recorded a deeper mark of the fear transmitted to me through my mother's shuddering body, which she used as a wall to protect me.*

Sterne's family spoke Yiddish in the home, but not on the street. It was risky to be identified as a Jew. Raphael Soyer recalls one such incident.

> *My father came home one evening out of breath and upset. When my mother asked him what had happened, he told her, and I overheard, that two drunken peasants walking behind him said, "There goes a Jew, let's beat him up!" "What did you do?" asked my mother. "I made big strides." My all-powerful father sank in my estimation.*

Not only Jews but all Russians of liberal or radical thought lived in the shadow of fear. The secret police were everywhere. The sound of soldiers on the street, the midnight knock on the door, made the heart race madly.

For Jews of that generation, life was a round of relentless persecution. Maurice Sterne's father died when the boy was seven; his mother got a job teaching in Moscow. Was the great city any better than little Libau? Only in the small and poverty-stricken Jewish ghetto district could the boy walk without fear of some derisive voice calling, "Jew! Jew!" At ten, Maurice entered a polytechnic school. "For the first time in my life," he said, "my classmates were not Jewish and until I was befriended by a big boy I was teased and tormented for being a Jew."

Maurice did well enough to earn a scholarship to the art academy. But only two days later the newspapers announced that all but a small number of selected Jews had to leave Moscow. The Jews were stunned. They did not know where to go, for many other parts of Russia were being closed off to them. Quickly they had to dispose of their homes, their belongings, their businesses, take any price and find ways and means of getting out. But to go where?

In St. Petersburg too, the Jews were kicked out. One of them, with desperate humor, went to Gresser, the chief of police, and said to him: "You leave the dogs in St. Petersburg. Well, I have eight children to feed, I have great difficulty in making a living. Let me remain here, and I will go on all fours like the dogs!"

"No," replied the police chief, "you are a Jew, you are less than a dog. Turn Christian."

In Warsaw the colonel commanding the garrison made a short speech to his troops:

> *Soldiers! Russia, our Little Mother, is passing through sad times. Wicked people, disturbers of the peace and Socialists, wish to divide up our country, and have even already begun to excite our brave troops, spreading their doctrine amongst the faithful servants of our Little Father, the Czar. Most of these agitators are Jews. . . .*
>
> *Remember them, my brothers, who your enemies are, and exterminate them everywhere, whenever you have the opportunity. . . . Remember that we are living in a state of siege, and the more each of you exterminates his enemies, the greater will be his reward.*

That evening a company commander came into the barracks and spoke to his men, piling more fuel on the fire his colonel had lit:

> *All the misfortunes which have befallen our country come exclusively from the Jews, who drink our blood, and yet pass for friends of the moujik and the Russian working man. But do not believe it! Mochka [he pointed*

to a Jewish soldier], he is your enemy, and I, a Russian
and Orthodox gentleman, I warn you. Do not believe
Mochka! Spit in his face!

The soldiers surrounded the Jew and carried out literally
the order of their commander. When Mochka could stand
it no longer, he struck back, was court-martialed, and sent
to military prison.

Such anti-Semitism was easily transformed into pogroms. These violent outbreaks against the Jews were ancient history in Russia. One of the earliest recorded goes
back to the year 1113, when the Jews of Kiev were attacked
and pillaged. In the sixteenth century Ivan the Terrible
ordered thousands of Jews to be drowned when they refused to abandon their faith and accept Christianity. In
1871 the Jews of Odessa suffered a pogrom, supposedly
caused by some Jew breaking a cross in a Greek Orthodox
church. A similar legend was the excuse for a Warsaw
pogrom in the same period.

But it was in the 1880s that pogroms by the hundreds
overwhelmed the Jewish population of Russia. This time
the authorities invented a new explanation: it seems that
the peasants and workers had been enslaved by the Jews,
and were rising up against their exploiters. The truth, of
course, was that the economic misery of the Russian people
was only the inevitable result of the brutal serfdom in
which Russia's rulers had held them for centuries, long
after the rest of Europe was moving into modern times. To
divert the blame for oppression from themselves, the Czar,
the nobility, and the landlords made the Jews the scape-
goat.

Russian radicals, driven to terrorism by their failure to
make any progress in winning basic reforms, killed the Czar

with a bomb in 1881. The result was only to make things worse. Six weeks after the assassination the authorities unleashed a pogrom in Elisavetgrad, where 15,000 Jews lived. The police and the military stood by, watching, while drunken mobs burned down homes, looted shops, raped women, and mutilated and murdered Jews regardless of age or sex. The rage to kill Jews, incited by the government-supported press, swept through 160 cities and villages in the next few weeks.

As the news of the pogroms reached communities at some distance from the scenes of horror, the effect upon the Jews was terrible. It became clear to them that the Jewish people had been virtually outlawed, and that no one would dare raise a hand in their defense. Shmarya Levin describes the mood in his town of Swislowitz.

No pogrom occurred in Swislowitz, but the terror of the pogrom was suspended almost visibly over our heads. There were times when we envied the cities that had already suffered the pogrom. "Better an end with terror than a terror without end." The fear that would not be abjured, the uncertainty that haunted us in the home and in the streets, the momentary expectation of the storm that did not break—this is a species of mental torment that cannot be described. The Jews of Swislowitz went around, as I remember, like shadows of themselves. They could not lie down and die; there was their daily bread to earn for themselves and their families, and pitifully small as their needs were, they could not satisfy them without maintaining their usual contact with the Gentiles. The contact was traditional, intimate. True, these Gentiles were our own village folk; but all that belonged to yesterday. Who could tell what deadly

*thoughts were theirs today? The volcano, too, is peaceful
just one moment before it breaks out.*

The sight of mobs clubbing down Jews in the streets
forced a great change in the attitude of many Russian Jews.
The government, they saw, had openly encouraged the
pogromists. And every sector of society had applauded, or
remained silent. The Jewish liberals and radicals, who had
thought progress inevitable, that education would lead to
reform, that Jews would win emancipation and equality,
suddenly recognized that to most Russians the Jew was a
despised outsider, an enemy to be gotten rid of by any
means.

In Kiev, where the Jewish quarter had been devastated
by a pogrom, a day of fasting and prayer was proclaimed by
the rabbis. The synagogues were filled with weeping victims. Suddenly a group of young men entered one of them,
and the crowd fell silent. The newcomers, all Jews, were
students of the University of St. Vladimir, rarely seen at
worship. Their leader spoke:

> *Brethren, we are a committee of the Jewish students
> of the university, sent to clasp hands with you and to
> mingle our tears with your tears. We are here to say to
> you, "We are your brothers; Jews like yourselves, like our
> fathers!" We have striven to adopt the language and
> manners of our Christian fellow countrymen, we have
> brought ourselves up to an ardent love of their literature,
> of their culture, of their progress. We have tried to per-
> suade ourselves that we are children of Mother Russia.
> Alas! we have been in error. The terrible events which
> have called forth this fast and these tears have aroused us
> from our dream. The voice of the blood of our outraged*

brothers and sisters cries unto us that we are only strang-
ers in the land which we have been used to call our
home; that we are only stepchildren here, waifs to be
trampled upon and dishonored.

There is no hope for Israel in Russia. The salvation of
the downtrodden people lies in other parts—in a land
beyond the seas, which knows no distinction of race or
faith, which is a mother to Jew and Gentile alike. In the
great republic is our redemption from the brutalities and
ignominies to which we are subjected in our birthplace.
In America we shall find rest; the stars and stripes will
wave over the true home of our people.

To America, brethren! To America!

To America they went. At first in a trickle, then in a
torrent. Four million Jews left Eastern Europe between
1880 and 1924. Over three million of them came to the
United States. Because of that heavy immigration, the Jewish population of the United States increased at a more
rapid rate in that period than the population as a whole.
The vast majority of Americans of Jewish descent today
stem from that immigration.

That they suffered from pogroms is only part of the
truth. They knew less violent forms of persecution too.
Tens of thousands of Jews were injured or killed in the
pogroms of the early 1880s, and many more in the waves of
pogroms that broke in 1903, in 1905, in 1919–20. Millions
of others were the victims of a "cold" pogrom. This was the
ever-growing body of restrictive laws directed against the
Jews. Long before, they had been penned up in the provinces of western and southwestern Russia, in an area
called the Pale of Settlement. Not content with isolating

95 percent of the Jews in this huge ghetto, the Czars humiliated and hounded them with hundreds of restrictions. One of the heaviest burdens was military conscription for a term of twenty-five years or more, with no chance to rise above private. Quotas barred all but a few Jews from the schools and universities. In 1886 Jews had little choice not only where they could live but in how they could earn a living. A small number managed to achieve wealth, but the vast mass of Jews starved in the villages (the *shtetls*) or the city slums. By the 1880s the four million Jews of Russia were a desperate, driven people. Across the Russian border, in the Austro-Hungarian provinces of Galicia and Bukovina, the Jews were almost as badly off. They too suffered great poverty, although their political and civil disabilities were lighter.

So they left home: one out of every three Jews in Eastern Europe. Of course, they were not the only ones to pick up and go. The whole continent of Europe was on the move in that century. The Jews were a part of that wandering. Between 1830 and 1930, forty million Europeans came to the New World. Thirty million of them arrived after 1880, and most of these were Slavs, Italians, and Jews out of Southern and Eastern Europe.

It is hard to grasp the vast scale of that migration. It was the biggest movement of peoples in world history. It followed the paths of promise, which led westward. They came—no matter from where—for similar reasons. They wanted to climb out of poverty, to break free of political oppression, to crack the mold of class, to worship as they pleased.

It was the people of the more advanced countries of Eastern and Central Europe who moved first. Then came the less developed Eastern and Southern countries, especially when cheaper rail and ship passage made flight easier. By the early 1900s, 1.5 million people were leaving Eastern and Southern Europe each year.

This was the mass migration which the Jews joined.

2 | To Go— or Not to Go

What is it like to pull up roots in your native land and seek a home in a strange place? What kind of person can do it?

Not everyone: that's clear. If one out of every three Jews in Eastern Europe migrated to America, it means two out of every three stayed where they were. Twice as many, then, decided not to leave, or never even thought of going.

What was the difference between the two groups? All, or nearly all, shared the same problems, felt the same pressures of poverty and persecution. How then do we account for the decision to go or not to go?

A look at the nature and condition of the Jews in Eastern Europe may help explain why. In 1800 the region held half the Jews of the world. Expelled from Western Europe in the centuries roughly between 1500 and 1800, the majority of Jews had moved east of the Rhine, chiefly to Polish territory. When that kingdom was dismembered by its warring neighbors, the Jews fell under Russian, Prussian, or Austro-Hungarian rule.

Most Jews were Orthodox then. They gloried in their separateness, writes Moses Rischin.

Rendered conspicuous by their dress, language and customs, and confined in their occupations and habitat, they knew they were Jews, anchored in religious traditions by their needs, their convictions, their communal life, and the state of the surrounding peasantry.

Adversity fashioned an inner existence that flamed up in direct proportion to the bleakness of an outer world that was shaped by rumors and realities of forced conversions and persecutions. Everyday life was transcended and embellished by a rich heritage of learning, liturgy, custom, and special observance. . . . Religious learning, the only kind of learning comprehensible to Jews, disciplined all. . . .

Much was tolerable on this earth, since this world was only an anteroom to the Hereafter and all Israel had a portion in the world to come. Whatever the strains between the well-to-do and the poor, all Jews shared in the pervasive personal and familial ties of the small towns. They were sustained by their sense of community, by a belief in a common destiny, and by a feeling of moral superiority to the surrounding world of lords and peasants.

But fresh social forces and the new ideas they gave rise to disrupted that self-contained Jewish world. The movement for Jewish enlightenment, called the Haskalah, which began in the eighteenth century, spread from the West to Poland and Russia. If Jewish customs and thought were modernized, argued its leaders, the Jews would be treated equally with non-Jews, and political emancipation would follow. The Western influence reached the larger cities first, then penetrated to smaller towns where Jewish youngsters from throughout Russia were schooled in renowned yeshivas. Unsettled youth were open to Haskalah teachings and the values of Russian and Western culture. When they found higher education and professional careers closed to them, many turned to radicalism. Socialist teachings reached not only the students but the emerging Jewish working class of the cities. The Bund was formed in 1897 to organize Jewish workers and to participate in independent political action. The Pale of Settlement, once lamented by the enlighteners as a stagnant pool where Jewish life had decayed, became "the hotbed of revolutionary work." Jewish nationalism, long dormant, was ignited by the torch of the pogromists. As Bundists demanded national cultural autonomy for Jews, the Zionists proposed plans to establish a homeland for the oppressed.

Jewish life in Eastern Europe had been in ferment, then, long before the wave of pogroms began in the 1880s. The inertia and immobility which characterized the community life of the Orthodox had begun to give way. Eastern European Jews, though only a handful, had made the long journey to North America as far back as the colonial period. With the beginning of Haskalah, with the introduction of military conscription, with the uprooting of Jews by edicts of expulsion, larger numbers began to flee abroad.

What made the early emigrants think of America? Many learned about it in the 1840s from *Zofnath Paaneach*, a Yiddish translation of J. H. Campe's German book about the discovery of America. "The Columbus," as they referred to it, became so popular "that almost all Jews read it," recalls A. B. Gotlober in his memoirs. There were penny booklets too which circulated the legend of an America whose streets were paved with gold.

Little of practical use was learned from such books, but

they stirred a hunger for more knowledge about America, and brought it closer to mind. By the 1840s Jews near the western borders were crossing over into Germany and some moved on from there to America. One Jewish writer of that time, Dr. S. Ettinger, fictionalized the adventures of Polish and Galician Jews who went to America and sometimes returned, usually to marry a home-town girl. Soon after, there was a book by the enormously popular Yiddish novelist of Vilna, I. M. Dick; he told the story of a forgotten relative who made a fortune in America and bequeathed it to the village teacher Reb Khaykel Yente of Tsyusk, the hero of the tale. The shipping agents drummed up business by distributing handbills on the wonders of life in the Golden Land. The slogan *"Auf zu Amerika!"* was heard in Austria-Hungary now. Before the American Civil War the records show Eastern European Jews living in such places as Utica, Rochester, New Orleans, Chicago, San Francisco, Los Angeles. By 1860 there were perhaps 15,000 of them in New York City.

The numbers swelled in the 1860s and 1870s. Alexander II, who began his reign (1855–81) as a liberal, lifted some of the restrictions on the Jews and freed the peasants from bondage. The economic development of Russia was stimulated. But denied enough land or capital to stand on their own, the peasants stayed poor. It was a dismal prospect for the Jewish tradesmen and artisans in the towns and villages who depended upon the peasants as customers. The peasants who gave up on the land moved to the cities, where they competed with the Jews for jobs. Epidemics of cholera, and famine caused by bad harvests, made life even worse. In 1869 an Odessa newspaper reported that "the situation of the hungry Jews is beyond imagination. Masses of them leave our fatherland and go to foreign countries to look for means to alleviate their hunger." From that year until 1881, about 3,000 Jews annually left Eastern Europe to seek new homes in America. Their mood is captured in the public appeal a group of Russian Jews made in 1880 to the Jews of America for help in emigrating:

> *Give us a chance in your great and glorious land of liberty, whose broad and trackless acres offer an asylum and a place for weary hearts but courageous souls, willing to toil and by the sweat of the brow earn our daily bread. Come, Brothers of Israel in America, come to our help.*
>
> *Give us the means to migrate to your shores. Let us touch with our feet the sacred soil of Washington, and with our freedom we shall become new-created for the great struggle of life.*
>
> *We do not fear work. We ask you but to land us on your free territory and send us to your Western lands, and we will answer for the rest.*

That open letter, printed in the press and in the *Congressional Record*, foreshadowed the enormous upheaval which began a year later, after the pogroms of 1881–82. A million and a half Russian Jews came to the United States in the span of the next thirty years.

Was it the result of the pogroms? It is too facile an answer to let it go at that. For in the same period more than 300,000 Jews came to America from Austria-Hungary, especially from its Galician province. And there were *no* pogroms or oppressive decrees in that region. Further, the same period saw a huge rise in the emigration of *non*-Jews from Eastern Europe. The Jewish and the non-Jewish emigrants shared two social conditions: a large rise in their population and a great worsening of their economic position. The Eastern European Jews experienced a fivefold increase in their population in the nineteenth century. The economy, failing to keep pace with such growth, left the masses worse off than before.

For some Jews the pogroms—hot and cold—may have been the final push to the decision to emigrate. But we are still left with the question: why did a third of them go, and the other two thirds stay? The historian Solomon Grayzel says many of those who stayed led "a spiritually satisfying life." Those were the Orthodox Jews who in the early years regarded America as profane. Later, when some did go, it was in large measure because their children went. The Orthodox were never a major part of the emigrants.

Another group who stayed, and openly disapproved of those who emigrated, were the enlightened, the assimilated, the affluent. They were distressed at the depth of the despair for the future which many Eastern European Jews felt. They urged the people to stay at home and improve themselves. They expected vocational training and diversification to win the Jews a stronger position in the economy. They believed modernized dress and the learning of Russian would bring social acceptance and cause anti-Semitism to disappear. (How wrong they were, history would soon demonstrate.)

Poverty, persecution—these economic and social facts conditioned the environment of the Eastern European Jews. But of themselves they did not oblige people to change their relationship to that environment. In this case, to make the grave decision to emigrate. The influence of environment upon each individual is indirect, mediated through his own temperament and ideas. Behind the decision of the Jews who emigrated were personal motives. And it is these which psychologists study in the hope of finding the link between social necessity and personal initiative. One researcher, Moses Kligsberg, himself an emigrant from Poland, analyzed a major source for the Jewish immigrant's own view of himself. He examined more than three hundred autobiographies written by Jewish immigrants in 1942 for the Yivo Institute for Jewish Research on the theme "Why I Left the Old Country, and What I Have Achieved in America." Most of the life stories represented the first mass immigration of the 1880s and 1890s. He concluded from the evidence that "the Jewish immigrant community in the United States is by and large a concentration of one social-psychological type, that is, the enterprising, activistic person with a strong individualistic attitude."

Not all of them, of course. There were many women and children who came to join husbands or fathers. And young men and women (some only teenagers) who came alone, and later brought over their parents, brothers, sisters. But Kligsberg felt certain that in America this type was "much more strongly represented than in any normal, settled Jewish community of Europe."

What moved this type of personality to emigrate? As adults, he said, they had a living ethnic heritage. Like all other immigrants, they came to America with personalities formed by a particular social and ethnic environment. Their Jewishness, the folkways and mores transmitted down the generations, was engrained in them. This Kligsberg calls the "passive" part of the immigrant's spiritual baggage. In addition, says Kligsberg, "he brought with him an active set of goals and aspirations: the Jewish immigrant came to America not merely to live with greater ease. He arrived with a powerful urge to achieve a goal, and with the dynamism appropriate to such an urge."

The Jewish immigrant may not have been aware of this; he may have voiced other reasons for leaving home, especially the standard explanation—hunger and pogroms. But the statistics show that Jewish emigration rose steadily during the relatively quiet years between the major pogrom periods of 1881–82 and 1903–4. More likely it was the superior economic conditions in the United States which attracted immigrants. For the trend of Jewish emigration to America paralleled the general flow of emigration by other ethnic groups.

Poverty does not fully account for the vast emigration any more than pogroms. The number who suffered from hunger was much greater than the number who emigrated. And there is evidence to show that not the poorest, but those a little better off, were the ones who emigrated.

What, then, explains the emigration of the Jews? Kligsberg attributes it, quite convincingly, to a unique guiding principle of Eastern European Jewish life. From earliest childhood, he says, Jews were confronted with one word: *takhlis*. The Hebrew word meant to them an end-goal: "What will the *takhlis* be?" That was always the important question.

A man realizes his full significance only in having achieved something, in having advanced in his environment, or at least in having maintained a high standard already achieved by his milieu. There can be neither meaning nor satisfaction in simply living one's life: one must achieve something, get somewhere. This, it can be said, is the core of the Jewish outlook for the individual.

Traditionally, Eastern European Jews sought *takhlis* in the spheres of learning, status, and financial security. The highest ideal parents held up to their children was to be a rabbi, a position that achieved all three goals. But when Jewish community life was breached by the rise of modern secular movements, and enlightened Jews began to look over the ghetto walls, they saw new paths to *takhlis* in the world beyond. It was then that the barriers to achievement which law and social custom had set up became more difficult to bear. For generations such restrictions had not mattered much in the daily life of the traditional Jew. He could aspire to become a rabbi or a merchant-scholar in spite of the wicked Gentiles. Now, however, when the modern Jew wanted to become a doctor, lawyer, engineer, professor, businessman, the denial of equal rights was felt as an intolerable insult to his self-respect.

For large numbers of the younger generation this Eastern European life came to have no *takhlis*. They looked to America, a land where they heard you could achieve *takhlis*. America promised the freedom to work your way up, to realize your own possibilities, and especially to school your children so that they could make their mark in the world.

It is this concept which enables us to understand the extraordinary "dynamism and zeal which the greatest number of Jewish immigrants manifested in America . . . the patience with which they bore the immensely difficult conditions of life—the sweatshops and tenements—and the fact that so small a number returned to the old country."

3 | Crossing in Steerage

The lure of America drew Jews from the most remote corners of Eastern Europe. In 1886, someone in Shavl, a village in the province of Kovno, sent this report to a Hebrew newspaper published in St. Petersburg:

> In the last ten years all local inhabitants were blinded and dreamt only about America with the gold and silver that is found there on the streets. This has increased the number of migrants. This year, in particular, a greater number of steamship tickets [shifskarten] were sold by salesmen. During the past week a substantial group of people, including fifty young persons, left for America and more were expected to go during the following week. Those who accompanied the immigrants wept on the way because they feared that their dear ones may not return or might encounter mishaps, or that some of their material support will be missing at home.

That vision of a golden America was satirized by Sholem Aleichem, the best-known Yiddish writer of modern times, who himself left the Old World for the New. Berl-Isaac, a character who is always letting his imagination run away with him, returns to Kasrilevka after a long stay in America. He tells the open-mouthed villagers of the wonders he has seen:

> To begin with, the country itself, a land flowing with milk and honey. People make plenty of money; you dig into money with both hands, you pick up gold by the shovelful! And as for "business," as they call it in America, there is so much of it that it just makes your head spin! You can do anything you like. You want a factory—so you have a factory; you want to, you push a pushcart; and if you don't, you peddle or go to work in a shop—it's a free country! You may starve or drop dead of hunger right in the street—there is nothing to prevent you, nobody will object.
>
> Then, the size of the cities! The width of the streets! The height of the buildings! They have a building there, they call it the Woolworth—so the top of its chimney-pot reaches into the clouds and even higher; it is said that this house has several hundred floors. You want to know, how do they climb up to the attic? By a ladder which they call an elevator. If you want somebody on the top floor, you sit down in the elevator early in the morning, so you get there towards sunset, just in time for your evening prayers. . . .
>
> Now take their life—it's all a rushing, a running, and a hustling. "Urry-hop" they call it there. Everything is in a hurry, and even when it comes to eating it is also done heels over head. You rush into a restaurant, order a schnapps, and as for the meal, I myself once saw a fellow being served something on a plate, something fresh,

alive, and kicking, and when he cut it in two, one half of it flew to one side and the other half to the other side, and the fellow was through with his lunch. . . .

Now, take their language. It's all turned upside down, as if for spite. If we call somebody a meat-merchant, they call him a butcher; if we say a houseowner, they say a landlord; a neighbor is a next-door-man or a next-door-woman; a hen is a chicken. Everything topsy-turvy. Once I asked the missus to buy a cock to kill for the Day of Atonement. So I couldn't explain to her what I wanted until I hit on the idea of telling her: "Buy me the gentleman of the chickens." This she understood and only then did she deliver herself of that fine word, "Alright," which means almost the same as when we say, "Be it so, why not? Sure, with the greatest of pleasure!"

No wonder, as Maurice Hindus put it, the villagers "out of sheer envy or incredulity might have been swung to support of Ivan the Fool, who had proclaimed the existence of America an invention and a fraud." Hindus, born in Russia in 1891, came to America at the age of fourteen and found it no fraud. In *Green Worlds* he describes the fantastic material abundance he saw. "The more meager the information of those who came," he said, "the more overwhelming was their joy in its discovery." And thinking of where they had come from:

Only then, in the light of this opulence of America, could they envisage the real destitution of the old village, of the whole world out of which they had come. What destitution! No socks, no handkerchiefs, no underwear, seldom enough soap, generations behind the New World, and with no visible hope of putting itself in a position to reach out for the knowledge, the energy, the ambition to transform itself to anything similar. How could it, steeped as it was in "the deep and horrible mud," as my mother would say, and all that it implied in daily living? It was hard enough to pull cows and horses and wagons and sometimes our own feet out of that black muck. To lift the whole scheme of living out of it would have required a power that was nowhere in sight, a power that could blow the mud off the face of the earth.

They did not transform their village, but many found the power in themselves to shake its mud from their feet and venture to America. Mary Antin, who was born in Polotzk, saw her father go off alone, without means, to a strange world where he had no friends, pioneering the way for his family. As they read together his first letter home, she sensed in it "more than the words seemed to say. There was an elation, a hint of triumph, such as had never been in my father's letters before. I cannot tell how I knew it. I felt a stirring, a straining. . . . My father was inspired by a vision. He saw something—he promised us something. It was this 'America.' "

His next letters told them that in America it was no disgrace to work at a trade. Cobbler and teacher alike were addressed as "Mister." And *all* the children—Jews and Gentiles, girls and boys—went to school. One day a letter arrived with a third-class steamer ticket for the family. Mary describes the effect upon the town.

Before sunset the news was all over Polotzk that Hannah Hayye had received a steamer ticket for America. Then they began to come. Friends and foes, distant relatives and new acquaintances, young and old, wise and foolish, debtors and creditors, and mere neighbors—from every quarter of the city, from both sides of the Dvina, from over the Polota, from nowhere—a steady stream of them poured into our street, both day and night, till the hour of our departure. And my mother gave audience. Her faded kerchief halfway off her head, her black ringlets straying, her apron often at her eyes, she received her guests in a rainbow of smiles and tears. She was the heroine of Polotzk, and she conducted herself appropriately. She gave her heart's thanks for the congratulations and blessings that poured in on her; ready tears for condolences; patient answers to monotonous questions; and handshakes and kisses and hugs she gave gratis.

What did they not ask, the eager, foolish, friendly people? They wanted to handle the ticket, and mother must read them what is written on it. How much did it cost? Was it all paid for? Were we going to have a foreign passport or did we intend to steal across the border? Were we not all going to have new dresses to travel in? Was it sure that we could get kosher food on the ship? And with the questions poured in suggestions and solid chunks of advice.

Planning for a trip today is infinitely easier than for those emigrants of a hundred years ago. Almost every inch of the earth's surface has been explored, mapped, and reported to the rest of the world by the instantaneous means of communications we now enjoy. Travel bureaus, public and private, advise us on transportation by car, rail, ship, or plane, inform us of schedules and costs, describe accommodations and make reservations, whether in the next county or on the far side of the globe. (All you need is cash or a credit card.)

It was altogether different back in the 1880s. There were

no automobiles or airplanes. Passage across land was by foot, horse and wagon, carriage, or train. Across the ocean it was by sailing or steam vessel. Steam was beginning to take over from sail, although it would be another thirty years before sailing ships would almost disappear from the seas. The telegraph was the rapid communications link. There was neither radio nor television nor motion pictures. The telephone was just being installed in a handful of homes and the typewriter was almost as new.

Think of what it was like for a Jew in Eastern Europe back in that time. Finding everything going wrong, you make a great resolve to begin life all over again. The way to do that, you decide, is to start on new soil. You determine to emigrate to America. But how will you go from the Old World to the New? What route should you take? What season is it best to travel in? How will you get out of the country when the government restricts passports? What will it all cost? And where will you get the money? You mean to go alone, to prepare the way for your family to follow. How will they live while you are gone?

One of the young men who struggled with such decisions wrote:

> On a day in August I left Znamenka for America. Gershon, my father's partner, brought the horse and wagon to drive me to the station. When I began to say goodbye, I saw tears in my father's eyes and my mother fainted. My brothers and sisters were crying loudly. I was almost ready to stay at home. When my mother was brought to, I said that if she wished it, I would not go.
>
> "No," she said, "I shall faint again when they take you away to be a soldier—and, maybe, to war, and then you won't be able to stay."

My father, Gershon and I climbed on the wagon and drive off. Gershon was begging me not to go. "I served as a soldier," he said, "and am I not alive?"

I hurried into the train not to be seen. My father bought me a ticket to Kremenchug and gave me money. The bell rang for the third time, we kissed each other, and in another minute or two the train was leaving.

At Kremenchug he had to change for the train to Romny, and from there go to Vilna to meet the agent of those who were to smuggle him across the border into Germany. After paying the agent fifty-five rubles, he spent the night hidden in a garret. The next day, with twenty others gathered for the same purpose, he was taken by train to Shavli, where they went to the home of a driver who was to bring them over the border.

That evening we were crowded into a covered wagon. The driver went as fast as he could and we were well shaken and bounced about. Every three hours they changed the horses. In the morning we stopped at a house in Tovrick. The man in charge put some of us in the garret, some in the cellar, the women in the only room, and me and another, perhaps because we had complained least, into the privy in the yard.

In two hours we were ordered back into the wagon and told not to worry—the coast was clear. "Each of you will get a passport and when the soldier asks for it, just give it to him." I read mine: my name was Bassie Baila Hendler, female, sixty-seven years old, grey-haired, and so forth. I could not help laughing at what had become of me.

We came to a little bridge. A soldier shouted, "Halt!"

and said to the man sitting beside the driver, "How many have you there?"

"Twenty-one."

"Have all passports?"

"As always."

"Let me have them." The soldier climbed into the wagon and counted the passengers, took away their passports, counted them, and said, "Right. Twenty-one rubles." The agent gave him the money, the driver whipped the horses, and in two minutes we were in Germany. The passengers began to joke and laugh at what they had been through. At the railway station, I sent this telegram to my parents and uncle: "Merchandise arrived complete and satisfactory."

From the border he went by train to Memel, then Stettin, and finally Hamburg, where he boarded a steamer for America.

The father of Morris R. Cohen left his family in Neshwies, a town in White Russia, and journeyed to America. Morris and his mother followed later. They too paid an agent to get them across the border illegally. "So many people went to America that way that the enterprise was quite standardized," he said. Russian law at that time prohibited emigration. The majority had to pass the border secretly or by bribery. Later, happy to get rid of Jews, the government changed its policy.

The first wave of the mass emigration came immediately after the pogroms of 1881. As committees formed outside Russia to appeal for aid to the victims, Jews began making their way to the Austrian border town of Brody. Jewish leaders of Western Europe were anxious to help, but when the number of emigrants mounted daily, they feared the wave would engulf their own countries. They began urging the emigrants to head for America, "that vast, free and rich country where all who want to work can and will find a place."

Jewish leaders in New York were not eager to welcome the Eastern Europeans. They protested the attempts to direct the people in Brody to America. Then the Austrian government changed its liberal policy, and some 8,000 fugitives were forced to return to Russia.

Large-scale emigration was renewed in the early 1890s when anti-Jewish restrictions—the cold pogrom—were rapidly intensified. This time Jewish philanthropists abroad were better prepared to help. Again, however, they tried to turn the tide away from their own countries. Significant numbers did go to Canada, South Africa, Germany, England, Latin America, and Palestine. But most of the emigrants had their eyes fixed on the United States. The graph of Jewish immigration began with about 6,000 in 1881, doubled in the next year, rose to 32,000 by 1887, and 50,000 in 1891. In the decade before World War I (1904–14) the annual number went over the 100,000 mark. It peaked at almost 150,000 in 1906, 1907, and 1914. The number of arrivals totaled two million by 1914.

The hardships of the Atlantic crossing came on top of the risks taken in trying to cross the border illegally in order to reach the bewildering ports of Western Europe. Ahead lay the terrors of the unknown Atlantic and the miserable conditions imposed upon steerage passengers by greedy shipowners. By the time of the great Eastern European emigration steamships had shortened the length of the voyage. But it took a long time for the human needs of space, air, food, sleep, and privacy to be recognized in law. The immigrants were so much freight to the shipping lines, nothing more.

Sleeping quarters in steerage were compartments holding three hundred or more persons. Berths, six feet two

YIVO Institute for Jewish Research

From Hamburg, the German port, many East European Jews took ship for America. This poster announces direct steamship service to New York, lists the five boats and their captains, and boasts that no other line can offer the same comfort

inches long, were in two tiers, with two and a half feet of space above each berth. Only an iron pipe separated the berths. Think of each berth space as an oblong box: that was the immigrant's territory. The iron framework held a mattress and a pillow (stuffed with straw or seaweed) and often a life preserver was the substitute for a pillow. The blanket was usually so flimsy passengers had to sleep in their clothing to keep warm. Stewards never changed or cleaned the berths, even when voyages lasted sixteen days or more. There was no room for hand baggage. As almost everyone came with a few household belongings—pots and pans, the family samovar, a prized pillow—these had to be kept in the berth space. (The floor was forbidden.) There were no closets or hooks for clothing; it had to be piled someplace on the berth. Some lines handed out eating utensils, which the passengers used throughout the voyage, and these too must be placed somewhere in the berth, as well as any personal towels or toilet necessities.

The shippers allowed limited open deck space to steerage and often provided no dining rooms. The immigrants lined up for their food and ate it in their berths. Since no waste barrels or sick cans were supplied, the steerage floor was always damp and filthy and the air stank beyond endurance.

Samuel H. Cohen recalls some details of his trip across the Atlantic, made in the early 1880s.

On the first day I went to the mess counter for food, and was handed a chunk of white bread and herring which I took to my bunk. (Of course meat or soup, which was treife, *I would not take.) I bit into the bread. It tasted like chalk. The herring stunk. I threw it all away. . . . We dug out of Joseph's pack some of the hard tack and rock-like farmer cheese that one of our relations had supplied. We munched on that. The following day we did not need food. In fact we seemed to have plenty to give up. It was stormy. The boat rocked and shook. The portholes had to be closed to prevent flood. The smell of disinfectant stifled me. I kept tossing about. I stuck my head out of the bunk a little. A shower of vomit came down from the upper bunk on my face. . . .*

There was no privacy. Men, women and children were all mixed together. . . . Our greatest suffering was due to a scarcity of water. We all provided ourselves with a tin can to hold the water distributed every evening. It was all you could get until the following evening. After a few days out, the quantity that each one received was cut down, but it soon became generally known that for money, more water could be procured. That day I ate a piece of herring. Soon after, I drank all the water I had. The same evening I was burning up with thirst.

Some ships built the bunks in three tiers. Morris R. Cohen crossed on one such, the *Darmstadt*, which took fourteen days from Bremen to New York.

We were huddled together in the steerage literally like cattle—my mother, my sister and I sleeping in the middle tier, people being above us and below us as well as on the same level. Naturally we could not eat the food of the ship since it was not kosher. We only asked for hot water into which my mother used to put a bit of brandy and sugar to give it a taste. Towards the end of the trip when our bread was beginning to give out we

*applied to the ship's steward for bread, but the kind he
gave us was unbearably soggy. The hardships of the trip
began to tell on my mother, so that she took sick and
developed a fever.*

To diminish the discomforts and indignity of the crossing, the U.S. Immigration Commission of 1908–11 investigated steerage-class conditions. The investigators were dis-
guised as travelers and sent to Europe. Then they made the
return trip in steerage. Anna Herkner crossed the ocean
three times in steerage in 1908. In her report she describes
the conditions she observed. What struck her above all was
the entire lack of privacy for steerage passengers. People
were herded together in hundreds. They had to spend every
hour of the twenty-four, many days running, in the presence of so many others.

*The sleeping quarters were always a dismal, damp,
dirty and most unwholesome place. The air was heavy,
foul, and deadening to the spirit and the mind. Those
confined to these beds by reason of sickness soon lost all
energy, spirit, and ambition. . . . They continued to lie
in their bunks as though in a stupor.*

The washing and toilet rooms were quite as inadequate
as the sleeping and eating accommodations, she said. There
were eight toilets and eight washbasins for over two hundred women and children and the same ratio for the men.
The toilet seats were always wet and water often stood
inches deep on the floor. The immigrants had to rise at five
or earlier if they hoped to get into a washroom before
breakfast at seven. "It really was no wonder to me when
some finally gave up trying to keep clean." A thorough

washing of the body or even part of it was out of the
question; there were no bathtubs and to monopolize a
basin for more than a few moments was impossible. All the
human needs were miserably provided for, or else entirely
ignored, she said. It meant the steerage passenger would
"arrive at the journey's end with a mind unfit for healthy,
wholesome impressions and with a body weakened and
unfit for the hardships that are involved in the beginning of
life in a new land."

Just before docking, each woman was given a piece of
candy and each man a pipe and tobacco. The intention was
to sweeten the last memory of steerage. . . .

YIVO Institute for Jewish Research

A devout immigrant in prayer aboard ship

The women left behind by their men who went on ahead sometimes waited years for their steamship tickets to arrive from
America. In this song a young seamstress pleads for her lover to
write often.

Tsvey-dray yor vel ich oyf dir
  vartn,
Afile finef, iz mir oych keday.
Ich vel lebn nor mit dayne brive-
  lech,
Un mutshen vel ich mich baym
  shnayderay.

Two and three years I'll wait for
  you,
And even five, I'll also wait.
I shall live only with your letters,

And struggle along at my
  dressmaking.

Ich vel dich aroysbaleytn kayn
  mayne eltern
Un vel loyfn, oy, tsu dem vogzal,

Ich vel dich aroysbaleytn kayn
  amerike,
Un vel loyfn, oy, tsu dem vogzal,

I'll sneak out without my parents
  noticing
And run to see you off, oh, at the
  station,
I will see you off as you go to
  America,
And tears will pour like a
  stream from my eyes.

Nor betn, bet ich dich, mayn
  tayer zis-lebn,
Zolst dayn libe nit fargesn dort,

Zolst mir bald fun dir a yedi-e
  gebn,
Az hobn zol ich fun dir chotsh a
  vort.

But I beg you, oh, I beg of you,
  my own true love,
That you do not forget our love
  over there,
Send me a communication
  immediately,
So that I get word from you
  soon.

4 | The Green Ones Arrive

One of the first Eastern European Jews to arrive in the early 1880s was young Abraham Cahan. Long after, when he was the famous editor of the Yiddish daily, the *Forward*, he recalled how it felt to sail into New York Harbor.

The immigrant's arrival in his new home is like a second birth to him. Imagine a new-born babe in possession of a fully-developed intellect. Would it ever forget its entry into the world? Neither does the immigrant ever forget his entry into a country which is, to him, a new world in the profoundest sense of the term and in which he expects to spend the rest of his life. I conjure up the gorgeousness of the spectacle as it appeared to me on that clear June morning: the magnificent verdure of Staten Island, the tender blue of sea and sky, the dignified bustle of passing craft—above all, those floating, squatting, multitudinously windowed palaces which I subsequently learned to call ferries. It was all so utterly unlike anything I had ever seen or dreamed of before. It unfolded itself like a divine revelation. I was in a trance. . . .

"This, then, is America!" I exclaimed, mutely. The notion of something enchanted which the name had always evoked in me now seemed to be fully borne out.

The immigrants were ferried over to Castle Garden, originally a fort built just before the War of 1812 at the foot of Manhattan Island in Battery Park. Renamed Castle Garden ten years later, the great rotunda was used as a concert hall. In 1855 it became the country's first receiving station for immigrants. By the time Cahan arrived, nearly half a million immigrants were passing through it each year.

Until 1882 almost anyone could enter the country. Government policy had been "hands off." Immigrants could come as they pleased. Nothing was done to encourage or discourage them. That year Congress adopted the first national immigration law. Inspection of immigrants was to be carried out by state boards under uniform rules at all ports of entry. Undesirables were to be kept out. This meant prostitutes, Chinese "coolies," or "any convicts, lunatics, idiots, or any person unable to take care of himself without becoming a public charge." Shipping lines were taxed fifty cents per immigrant to cover the costs of running the landing depots and attached hospitals. (Seven out of every ten immigrants came through the port of New York; the others entered at Portland, Boston, Philadelphia, Baltimore, Key West, New Orleans, Galveston, and San Francisco.)

Castle Garden would survive as a landing depot only another ten years, when it was replaced by Ellis Island. But in its last decade it processed over five million immigrants, far too many for its facilities. One of those millions was I. Kopeloff, a young Russian Jew. His first impression:

Castle Garden, a large circular, rotunda-shaped build-ing, had the appearance, to my eyes, of the arsenal in the castle of Boberisk, or of its tower, and struck me with gloom. . . . The main hall was huge and barren, and gave off an uncanny coldness which produced in its in-habitants an involuntary oppression. One after another sighed and sighed . . . [It] was often so crowded, so jammed, that there was simply nowhere to sit by day, or any place to lie down at night—not even on the bare floor.

The filth was unendurable, so many packages, pillows, feather beds and foul clothing (often just plain rags) that each immigrant had dragged with him over the seas and clung to as if they were precious—all of this pro-vided great opportunity for vermin, those filthy little beasts, that crawled about freely and openly over the clutter and made life disagreeable. The constant scratch-ing and the distress of the little children touched one to the quick.

Failure to anticipate the tidal wave of immigration ac-counted for the overcrowding. But greed and inhumanity were responsible for many other abuses. It started back in the old country when unsuspecting immigrants paid second-class fares for subsequent steerage passage. On this side of the ocean, transfer agents demanded double the normal price to ship the immigrants' baggage, the railroads ex-tracted gross profits from the sale of tickets, money changers chopped down the going market rate, the tele-graph charged for messages that were never sent. Com-plaints piled up until the federal government decided to dispense with state control, take over the immigration process, and build a new center for New York.

To replace Castle Garden, the government chose a tiny blob of mud and sand lying in a shallow of New York Harbor. Workers had to double the three acres of Ellis Island with landfill in order to provide space for a substantial building. The two-story station constructed of wood was about 400 by 150 feet, and looked like a seaside hotel. Opened in 1892, the firetrap burned down in 1897 (no one was injured, luckily); it was replaced in 1900 by a new brick building. Again the planners guessed wrong, for they never expected the half-million annual immigration rate of the recent past would ever climb higher. It did. And for the next fifteen years, the newcomers had to fight fiercely for room, even though the island was eventually filled in to an area of twenty-one acres.

Surrounding the main building on Ellis Island were medical facilities, bathhouse, laundry, kitchens, dining room, and an electric power plant. With the new facilities came new regulations. The 1882 law was replaced with a more comprehensive one in 1891. Federal control was placed in the hands of a new Bureau of Immigration whose Superintendent reported to the Treasury Department. The stricter set of rules added new categories of "undesirables" —polygamists, people guilty of "moral turpitude," and people suffering from "a loathsome or contagious disease." A law of 1885 intended to keep out workers brought over under contract to employers was toughened. Aliens who came in illegally or who became public charges within a year of arrival were to be deported. (In 1904, over 8,000 aliens were deported.) The 1891 law was stiffened two years later by amendments.

In a single day Ellis Island sometimes handled as many as 7,000 immigrants. How did it manage it? Jacob Riis, a reporter, watched the newcomers in 1903 and told what he saw in *Century* magazine.

By the time the lighters are tied up at the Ellis Island wharf their human cargo is numbered and lettered in groups that correspond with like entries in the manifest, and so are marshaled upon and over the bridge that leads straight into the United States to the man with the pen who asks questions. When the crowd is great and pressing, they camp by squads in little stalls bearing their proprietary stamp, as it were, finding one another and being found when astray by the mystic letter that brings together in the close companionship of a common peril —the pen, one stroke of which can shut the gate against them—men and women who in another hour go their way, very likely never to meet or hear of one another again on earth. The sense of the impending trial sits visibly upon the waiting crowd. Here and there a masterful spirit strides boldly on; the mass huddle close, with more or less anxious look. Five minutes after it is over, eating their dinner in the big waiting-room, they present an entirely different appearance. Signs and numbers have disappeared. The groups are recasting themselves on lines of nationality and personal preference. . . .

Behind carefully guarded doors wait the "outs," the detained immigrants, for the word that will let down the bars or fix them in place immovably. The guard is for a double purpose: that no one shall enter or leave the detention room. . . . Here are the old, the stricken, waiting for friends able to keep them; the pitiful colony of women without the shield of a man's name in the hour of their greatest need; the young and pretty and thoughtless, for whom one sends up a silent prayer of thanksgiving at the thought of the mob at that other gate, yonder in Battery Park, beyond which Uncle Sam's strong hand reaches not to guide or guard. And the hopelessly bewildered are there, often enough exasperated at the restraint, which they cannot understand.

Harsh and discomforting as the inspection system at Ellis Island seemed to the immigrants, still, it was relatively efficient. The other major immigration ports—Boston, Philadelphia, Baltimore—were undermanned and chaotic.

Once accepted for entry, the immigrants heading out of New York were ticketed with the name of the route that was to carry them to their new homes. But even on this last leg of the long journey the immigrants were marked as prey for the greedy. Anna Herkner, the Immigration Commission's investigator, reported what happened in the room where she and the other immigrants were sorted according to the railroad by which they were to continue their journey.

A rough guard pushed me to the pen into which I belonged. A commissary clerk met me, led me to a spot where my baggage could be deposited, then to a counter, saying "Show your money." I was about to obey, as a steerage passenger obeys these commands given at so many points of his journey, when I concluded that this was the attempt to compel one to buy a box of provisions for his further journey. Many of the passengers had told me of it and warned me. I refused to show my money, saying I was going only to Baltimore and did not need provisions for so short a journey. The man continued shouting, thinking to force me into buying, until he spied someone else entering. Then he dropped me and ran for the new victim. . . . The immigrants are practically forced to buy these boxes, regardless of the length of their journey or their desires. . . .

Finally we were taken from here to our respective stations. We who were going on the _____ Line crossed in a ferry to a dingy, dirty, unventilated waiting room next to the _____ station in Jersey City. Here we waited from 6 o'clock in the evening until after 9. About 8 o'clock the attendant signaled us to go downstairs, showing our tickets as we went. We all expected we were to board the train, so anxiously hurried along, dragging our heavy and numerous hand baggage. The poor, travel-tired women and the sleepy little children were pitiful sights. Arrived at the bottom of the long stairs, we waited and waited, but there was no train.

At last they boarded a train and arrived in Philadelphia, halting in the middle of the yards because they had to change trains.

We piled out in the middle of the night, all laden down with baggage, the women having, in addition, sleeping and sleepy little children. A trainman guided this weary and dejected party along the car tracks through the sleet and snow over an endless distance, it seemed, to the station . . . to what evidently was a lounging room for section hands. We were locked in there for an hour and a half, when we were again led to the station to be put on a train. They assigned us to the smoker—women, children and all—and refused even to open the women's toilet for us, compelling us to use the men's. . . . What those immigrants who had to travel longer distances suffered can well be imagined from the experiences of this short journey.

The alien had little or no protection. Ignorant of the devices of fraud, he responded to friendly overtures, thinking everyone in this wonderful America was eager to help. Countless thousands were cheated at docks and on trains and boats, risked health and safety in wretched traveling conditions, and suffered painful losses at the hands of dishonest travel agents, lawyers, bankers, notaries, interpreters. The U.S. government only admitted the immigrant; he was on his own in everything else.

Take Maurice Hindus, who came to America in the autumn of 1905.

I arrived in New York wearing my best clothes—my Russian school uniform, black belted tunic, long trousers, and military cap with a black shiny visor. I must have been an outlandish sight, especially to children. They stared and laughed at me, and overnight my eldest brother, who had come ahead of us and had paid for our ship tickets, changed me into an American outfit: knee pants, jacket, black stockings, and a soft cap. Proudly I walked the streets, but inwardly I felt bewilderingly alien, for no two worlds could have been more stupendously unlike than the mud-sodden village from which I had been uprooted and the towering New York into which I was flung. . . .

The overpowering surprises of New York—the tall buildings, incredibly tall, the gas and electric lights that banished night from the streets, the horsecars and trolleys that carried one wherever one chose to go and, marvel of marvels, the elevated trains thundering right over one's head. Least of all did rural or town Russia prepare me for the newsstands which sold enormous-sized dailies at a penny each—an unbelievably low price for so much paper. . . .

The streets lured me irresistibly. They were my first American school. It was in the streets that I saw for the first time Negroes, Chinese, Italians, Hungarians, Irish, others of the multitude of nationalities that made up New York. I had read of these people and now I saw them in the flesh. I yearned to speak to them, to learn all I could about them: how they lived, what foods they ate, what books they read, what they talked about when they were by themselves, what they thought of the peoples among whom they lived, and how they differed from the muzhiks, the Jews, the intellectuals I had known in the Old World. But language was a barrier I couldn't hurdle—not yet. I contented myself with watching and wondering about them—the Chinese in the laundries, the Negroes as day laborers, the Irish as truck drivers, policemen, and saloonkeepers, the Italians as shoe-shiners, ice and coal carriers, peanut venders, and organ-grinders.

Abraham Cahan tells of the immigrant who rushes from Ellis Island to the heart of the Jewish East Side. Unlike Hindus, he wants first of all to see and be with other Jews.

The streets swarmed with Yiddish-speaking immigrants. The sign-boards were in English and Yiddish, some of them in Russian. The scurry and hustle of the people were not merely overwhelmingly greater, both in volume and intensity, than in my native town. It was of another sort. The swing and step of the pedestrians, the voices and manner of the street peddlers, and a hundred and one other things seemed to testify to far more self-confidence and energy, to larger ambitions and wider scopes, than did the appearance of the crowds in my birthplace.

The great thing was that these people were better dressed than the inhabitants of my town. The poorest looking man wore a hat (instead of a cap), a stiff collar and a necktie, and the poorest woman wore a hat or a bonnet. . . .

Many of the passersby paused to look at me with wistful smiles of curiosity.

"There goes a green one!" some of them exclaimed. . . .

I understood the phrase at once. And as a contemptuous quizzical appellation for a newly arrived, inexperienced immigrant, it stung me cruelly. As I went along I heard it again and again. "Poor fellow! He is a green one," these people seemed to say. "We are not, of course. We are Americanized."

5 | Sheeny!

The Jews flooding in from Eastern Europe arrived at a time when America was transforming itself into the foremost industrial nation of the world. Mechanization, which had begun in the 1850s, was given a tremendous boost by the Civil War. The agricultural society of the prewar era was changing beyond belief.

Take the year 1900—the midpoint of the new immigration wave and the beginning of another century—as a marker. The people first: their number stood at 76 million. It was a population in great flux. Although the free land of the frontier was gone, a continuous stream of people kept pouring into Texas, the Plains states, and the Pacific Coast. Even more people, however, were deserting the countryside and the small towns for the rising cities. Many were jobless farmhands, forced off the land by the new labor-saving machines.

Add to these changes the tidal wave of the new immigration from Southern and Eastern Europe. It was not only a huge addition to the American population in numbers but a spectacular shift in source. Fewer than before meant to settle on the land. They too saw the promise of a more abundant life in the great urban centers. (In the dime novels of the day the boys who made good did it in the cities.) In just one decade, 1880–90, the urban population soared from 14 to 22 million. By 1900 one out of every three Americans was a city dweller. In 1920 they would be the majority of the population.

Many of the immigrants who entered at the port of New York simply stayed there. The city rapidly doubled in size, reaching 3.5 million. The furious pace of urban growth created a need for the immigrants' labor. By 1900 over a third of all New Yorkers were foreign-born. Chicago experienced the same dizzying rise, reaching half New York's population, but with three fourths of its people foreign-born.

The older Americans saw in the newcomers a threat to the country's basic institutions. The coming of so many millions of strangers and in so short a period of time alarmed them. It was not the first time that immigrants were made to feel unwelcome. Nativism—distrust of newcomers—had taken root early in colonial times. Even the revolutionary Founding Fathers—Franklin, Jefferson, Hamilton—had argued against free immigration for fear that "foreign elements" would disrupt the new nation's life.

Sharp increases in immigration had begun with the arrival of the Irish in the pre-Civil War decades. It triggered an anti-Catholic hysteria. Cries went up of a "foreign conspiracy" engineered by the Pope to seize the United States. The Irish, who came poor, were treated with open contempt, called brutish, clannish, vicious. That did not prevent the young industrialism from making use of the cheap, plentiful labor the Irish provided, which could not be found easily among the older American stocks. For a generation or more the Irish did the dirtiest and hardest work. As they climbed the social scale, they were replaced by the much larger immigration which began in the 1880s.

With the huge numbers pouring in from Eastern and Southern Europe came a renewal of nativism. Now it was not one but a dozen different ethnic groups arriving. Their strange languages, religions (mostly Greek Orthodox, Roman Catholic, and Jewish), social customs, and political backgrounds again made the dominant white Anglo-Saxon Protestants fearful and hostile. Some believed the era of American expansion had ended and that there would be no place for the newcomers. Then, disappointed and hungry, they would overturn the country by revolution. Another argument ran that these immigrants were different from the earlier ones and inferior, incapable of adjusting to American life. Even the reformer Henry George saw the new immigration as a process of "dumping garbage" on American shores. And Emma Lazarus, the Jewish poet, though a friend to the immigrants, in her famous sonnet spoke of them as "wretched refuse."

Racial theories, which had recently sprung into virulent life in Europe, spread rapidly in America. The new pseudo-science held the "Nordic" or "Aryan" stock to be superior, and the Southern and Eastern European peoples fit only to serve the master races. On the one hand, it was charged that the newcomers could never be absorbed into the mainstream. And on the other, that if they were, by intermarriage, it would destroy the character of the nation and bring chaos and ruin.

A harsh selfishness marked the treatment of all minorities in that age. The Indians, ruthlessly exploited from the beginning, were now herded onto reservations. The limited gains the emancipated blacks had made during the brief Reconstruction era were steadily eroded. The Mexicans laboring in the West were dismissed as "dirty greasers." The Chinese, "those yellow rascals" who had been sweated in the mines and in the building of the railroads, were suddenly shut out of America completely by the Chinese Exclusion Act of 1882.

When hard times came—the depressions of 1873 and 1893—many citizens, frantic with fear of losing what they had, made scapegoats of the foreign and the weak. The new middle class especially was prone to hysteria under the erratic pressures of rapid industrialization and urbanization. The popular culture of the period illustrates their insecurity. The Currier & Ives lithographs and the small colored trade cards given away to promote consumer products made the Irish, the blacks, and the Chinese the targets of a racist put-down humor.

The merchants, professionals, white-collar workers, and skilled mechanics felt the rising tide of immigration threatened their hard-won status. Practically all these newcomers were job seekers, over 60 percent were males, and the same percentage were young (between fifteen and forty). Worse in the eyes of the established wage earners was the fact that most of the immigrants were poor and unskilled. Eager for jobs and experience, the newcomers would "work for almost nothing and seem to be able to live on wind—something which I cannot do," as one worker put it. Union men therefore objected to unlimited immigration. Their leaders thought it would be almost impossible to organize people who spoke so many different tongues. The immigrants did prove hard to organize in some cases, and occasionally they were used to scab. But the trade unions themselves shared the blame so long as they refused to recruit the masses of unskilled workers.

It was during these years that American Jews began to encounter greater social anti-Semitism. It was part of the general rise in anti-foreign feeling. Many immigrant groups were attacked, some worse than the Jews. Catholics as a whole were the target of an organized opposition which the anti-Semites never developed to the same degree. And Italians were the victims of far more violence. Still, Jews were not safe from fist or rock. William Zorach recalls the treatment his family received on the streets of Cleveland.

When one of my brothers came home from work, he was attacked and beaten up by a bunch of rowdies. He said nothing, but when this began happening every night, he became more and more miserable and finally told my father. My father and a couple of my older brothers went out that night. They took crowbars and went after this gang. We heard the crowbars flying and clanking around the street. After that my brother had no more trouble.

My father used to be harassed and attacked and stoned. Boys yelled "Sheeny" at him on the streets. I remember some kids getting him into their yard to buy a sack of junk. It was supposed to be iron, but when he looked in, it was only rocks. When he wouldn't fall for it, they began pelting him with the rocks. He ran down the street yelling, with the kids after him. . . . I was miserable for my father and myself.

In the Brownsville neighborhood of Brooklyn, Morris Cohen ran up against anti-Semitism as he walked to school.

Beyond Dean Street I passed a number of houses inhabited by Germans who delighted to set their young children on me, yelling "Sheeny" and running after me as if they were going to attack me from the rear. When I turned around they would retreat, but as soon as I resumed my walk they would return to their annoying pastime. One day I became so irritated that I ran after one of the youngsters and slapped his face. At once, his older brother came out of the house and gave me a good thrashing for hitting someone below my size. But the total result was satisfactory for the youngsters thereafter left me alone.

Until the Civil War, anti-Semitism in the United States had been only sporadic. There were but 150,000 Jews in America in 1860. Most Americans never saw and probably never thought about them. Attacks upon Jews were usually directed against individuals, often by those who envied or competed with them. Jews who earned prominence in any field were the more likely to be attacked for their origins or faith. Nevertheless, Jews were capable of winning public support, as evidenced by the election of a number to public office of both high and low degree.

America's Jewry was different from other Jewries, younger by far (except now for Israel), and with a history that began without the problem of Emancipation that faced other Jewries in modern times. From the founding of the United States the Jews were guaranteed freedom of religion and equal rights. It was a status they never had seriously to contest. The question of Emancipation of the Jews has therefore never become an issue dividing the American people. Anti-Semitism may be found in every class and in every political persuasion, from right to left. But no one has built a political movement upon it (as in France, Germany, Poland, Russia) with demands that Jews be made second-class citizens, expelled, or exterminated. Anti-Semitism has been more of a social or cultural phenomenon, casual, impulsive, lacking any long-range radical goals.

The dormant prejudice is likely to be awakened by vast national upheavals, such as the Civil War. In both North and South, Jews were made the scapegoats for hurts suffered during the long agony of the struggle over slavery. And for the first and only time in American history, the Jews as a *people* were punished by anti-Semitism. The notorious episode revolved around the action of General U. S. Grant in expelling the Jews as a class from an occupied Southern region where speculators were profiteering on cotton. Far more non-Jews than Jews were guilty of the corruption, but Grant closed his eyes to the others. President Lincoln revoked the unjust order when Jews bombarded the White House with protests.

Jewish stereotypes that originated abroad and in much earlier times found their way to America. They were basically of two kinds, the religious and the economic, and as is often true of stereotypes, expressed mixed feelings. In the religious stereotype the Jews were seen as God's Chosen People, miraculously preserved to carry out His divine purpose. But at the same time they were held to be the deserving victims of His wrath as the "betrayers" of Christ.

In the economic stereotype the Jews were held to be of keen and resourceful intelligence, a constructive and enterprising force in the development of the economy. But again, at the same time, they were portrayed as grasping, greedy, and unscrupulous (the Shylock image). The religious stereotype faded to a degree in America, but the negative side of the economic stereotype gained ground rapidly after the Civil War. For it was now that the German Jews, who had made the first mass migration of Jews to America beginning in the 1830s, became conspicuous. In less than one generation many had risen from rags to riches. Starting often as peddlers, they became leading retail merchants, bankers, manufacturers. Perhaps no other immigrant group had made good so fast. Their ambition and their success made them easy targets. The common ethnic stereotypes stress inferiority, but the Jews left an opposite impression, of superior capacity. Anti-Semites soon twisted this into "the overbearing ability of Jews to gain advantage in American life."

The middle- and upper-class Gentiles, themselves scrambling for place and power among the nouveaux riches of the Gilded Age, began to exclude the Jews from summer resorts, neighborhoods, clubs, private schools. In 1881 Nina Morais, a Philadelphia Jew, described what was happening.

> The provident hotel-keeper avoids the contact of the Hebrew purse; the little child in school finds no room for the Jew in the game at recess; the man of business, whose relations with an Israelite have been close and honorable, gives vent to a passing feeling of displeasure in the reproach of "Jews." In social and professional clubs, the "Jew" is blackballed. "Jew" is the text of the political opposition orator. The liberal-minded host tells his guests, with an apologetic air, that the stranger among them "is a Jew, but quite a cultured man." An agreeable companion is spoken of as "a good fellow, if he

is a Jew." The merchant who cheats his creditors, the criminal in the prisoner's dock, is a civil offender if he belongs to the Baptist or Episcopal denomination, but if he comes of Hebrew blood, Judaism is made responsible for fraud and theft. Jew, Jew, Jew is the one all-comprehensive charge.

One magazine, *The Journalist*, always referred to Joseph Pulitzer, the innovative publisher of the New York *World*, as "Jewseph Pulitzer." The editor remarked that Pulitzer "is a smart businessman because he is a Jew and has the commercial instincts of his race very sharply developed within him."

At first the plight of the Jews in Czarist Russia evoked sympathy among Americans. When news of the tens of thousands of Jews injured or killed in the pogroms of 1881–82 appeared in the press, seventy-five non-Jewish groups held a protest meeting in New York City. But only a couple of months later the influential magazine *Century* ran an article by a Russian which sought to justify the pogroms. The nasty Jews, it seemed, had brought the pogroms upon themselves. Although Emma Lazarus replied to the slander in the next issue, the original article was a sign that the intellectuals too were infected with anti-Semitism.

Emma Lazarus stood apart from the many German-American Jews who were hostile to the Eastern European Jews. The German Jews felt they had barely established themselves and here was a mass migration of "outlandish foreigners" threatening to wreck everything they had created. The Yiddish of the newcomers they ridiculed as a "piggish jargon." The business competition that rapidly

developed between the two groups sharpened the antagonism. The Germans spoke contemptuously of their Russian
rivals, many of whose names ended in "ki," as kikes.

It was for such reasons that the established Jewry—the
"uptown Jews"—proposed limits on the immigration of
the Eastern Europeans. They also feared a huge financial
burden would be imposed upon them for the care of the
immigrants. The United Hebrew Charities, formed in 1874
for the relief of needy Jews, returned to Europe all immigrant Jews incapable of earning a living here. Needy immigrants who stayed looked to the charities for help, but there
were not enough funds to take care of all. By the 1890s,
however, there was a readier acceptance of the newcomers.
Partly because of a deepening sense of obligation to the less
fortunate members of the faith. In 1884 the Hebrew Shel-
tering House Association was founded on the Lower East
Side to befriend the Jews on arrival. It provided shelter and
food, helped locate relatives and friends, and got jobs. In
1909 it merged with the Hebrew Immigrant Aid Society.
The Jewish welfare program expanded to national and international scope. The earlier arrivals joined in with manpower and money, believing it their duty to help the next
ones to get started. Wherever they found themselves, religious, cultural, and historical ties bound Jews together.

6 | Tenements and Strangers

One square mile on the Lower East Side of New York became the America of the Eastern European Jews—the "downtown Jews." It was to New York that most of the immigrants came, and in New York that they stayed. Before the 1870s there was no truly distinct Jewish neighborhood in the city. It began when the German Jews set up their wholesale and retail enterprises in lower Manhattan. Both Grand Street and Canal Street were packed with their garment shops. Many of the Polish Jews who were among the first Eastern Europeans to come, were skilled tailors. They secured work from the German Jews and found it convenient to settle nearby, at the foot of Canal Street. Here, at Rutgers Square, four major arteries met—Canal, East Broadway, Rutgers, and Essex. When the Russian Jews began arriving in 1882, they were drawn to the same neighborhood. It became the heart of the Jewish quarter.

There were many such immigrant enclaves in New York; it was natural for the newcomers to collect in neighborhoods where they could feel at home with their own. There were a dozen different ethnic colonies—Irish and German,

Austrian and Hungarian, Bohemian and Italian, French and English. By the 1890s, the Lower East Side had become largely Eastern European Jewish. Older New Yorkers, crowded by the newer, left for less congested corners of Greater New York. The city stretched its limits beyond Manhattan, and by 1898 embraced the Bronx, Brooklyn, Queens, and Richmond, completing the metropolis we know today.

One of the immigrant boys whose family settled on the Lower East Side was Samuel Chotzinoff. He gives us the view from Rutgers Square.

East Broadway was a wide thoroughfare. Our apartment on the third floor of a house on the corner of Rutgers Street overlooked a large square, or rather oblong, adorned by a large black marble fountain rising in several tiers. I could sense the possibilities of the neighborhood. For, besides the fountain, all the buildings on the west side of East Broadway, extending from Essex to Jefferson streets, had been razed for the eventual construction of a park, and the debris offered the very terrain for possible war games, with rival armies marching and counter-marching and striving to gain certain desirable heights. . . .

Looking up Rutgers Street toward the east, there was the river in the distance, with boats of every description plying up and down. Huge warehouses near the water's edge were forever discharging crates and barrels with mysterious contents, and at night one could sit on the large empty trucks parked on the wharves and watch the river and the lights from Brooklyn across it. Within walking distance were splendors like Brooklyn Bridge, the City Hall, and the Post Office. The mysterious alleys of Chinatown were no more than half a mile away. Certainly East Broadway, at its meeting with Rutgers Square, was the center of the universe.

The Jews clustered in neighborhoods according to the parts of Eastern Europe they had come from. Moses Rischin mapped a cultural geography of the Lower East Side, street by street.

> *Hungarians were settled in the northernmost portion above Houston Street, along the numbered streets between Avenue B and the East River, once indisputably Kleindeutschland. Galicians lived to the south, between Houston and Broome, east of Clinton, on Attorney, Ridge, Pitt, Willett, and the cross streets. To the west lay the most congested Rumanian quarter, "in the very thick of the battle for breath," on Chrystie, Forsyth, Eldridge, and Allen streets, flanked by Houston Street to the north and Grand Street to the south, with the Bowery gridironed by the overhead elevated to the west.*
>
> *After 1907 Levantines, last on the scene and even stranger than the rest, for they were alien to Yiddish, settled between Allen and Chrystie streets among the Rumanians with whom they seemed to have closest affinity. The remainder of the great Jewish quarter, from Grand Street reaching south to Monroe, was the preserve of the Russians—those from Russian Poland, Lithuania, Byelorussia, and the Ukraine—the most numerous and heterogeneous of the Jewries of Eastern Europe.*

The immigrants sailing into the port of New York in the early 1880s saw nothing like the skyline of today. The

Statue of Liberty would not be erected until 1886, Ellis Island was nothing but a blob of mud, and the biggest building in town was only ten stories tall. North of Battery Park, church spires pierced the sky, and beyond them were visible the treetops of rural Manhattan. Off to the right soared the towers of the new Brooklyn Bridge, spanning the East River. The city was just about to enter its most explosive era of expansion. . . . The upward thrust of the skyline began in 1882 with the erection of the Washington Building at No. 1 Broadway, "the first skyscraper." In the 1890s the profile of downtown New York changed enormously, as one after another new steel-skeleton buildings competed for the title of "the tallest building in the world."

The Lower East Side could lay claim to a different distinction: the most crowded slum district in the city, and probably in the world. The young Maurice Hindus, fresh from rural Russia, was enthralled by it.

> *I loved to wander the streets of the Lower East Side and get lost in the adventure. The noisy bustling crowds fascinated me, everyone so feverishly busy. Immigrants mostly, they seemed like a new race in the world, different in manners and behavior from the people I had known on the other side of the ocean. Energetic and purposeful, they were astonishingly informal: well-to-do shopkeepers walked around without coats, sometimes with shirt sleeves rolled up as no member of their profession would deign to do in the scruffy little city where I had gone to school. Overalled janitors, icemen, peddlers tipped their caps to nobody—the very custom was unknown, and so was hand-kissing.*

*Several blocks from where we lived was roaring, bus-
tling Hester Street. The pavement was lined with stalls
and pushcarts, and men with cribs or baskets suspended
on leather straps from their necks pushed their way
along, crying their wares—needles, thread, shoelaces,
soap, socks—like hawkers in a Russian bazaar. The
filthiest section of the neighborhood, it was also the
busiest and most exciting. Customers haggled over prices
as violently and abusively as muzhiks. Shopkeepers
grabbed the arms of passers-by and with torrents of ca-
jolery endeavored to pull them inside their stores, curs-
ing those who had escaped their clutching hands. Russian or Polish women, obviously peasants, struggled
through the crowds calling for someone to rescue them
from clinging Hungarian or Romanian peddlers or shopkeepers whose language they didn't understand. All was
bedlam, a cacophony of voices, the Yiddish dialects of
Eastern Europe rising above all others. Here the Old
World strove loudly against the New with all its undis-
ciplined brashness, a product of the ruthless century-old
struggle for survival.*

New York was growing too fast for its inhabitants to
either understand or control it. The Tenth Ward, the center of the factory district on the Lower East Side, was the
most crowded in the city, with 523.6 inhabitants per acre.
(Manhattan as a whole averaged 114 per acre, and the
entire city 60 per acre.) The health officers called it the
"typhus ward" and to the Bureau of Vital Statistics it was
the "suicide ward." People were jammed more densely into
its tenements than anywhere else in the world, including
the notorious slums of London, India, and China.

Looking at Rivington Street, the English novelist Arnold Bennett said, "The architecture seemed to sweat humanity at every window and door." By 1914 the streets below Fourteenth held a sixth of the city's population—this on one eighty-second of New York's total land area.

The heavy influx of immigrants created a similar mosaic of crowded ethnic neighborhoods in many cities. But compare New York's density with other places. The Baltimore slums of 1890 held 7.71 persons per dwelling; Philadelphia held 7.34; Chicago 15.51; and New York—36.79! Plague-ridden Bombay was the only other place in the world to come close to New York's slums for congestion. And not really that close, for it held a third less people per acre.

From steerage quarters aboard ship, the immigrants came to slum tenements ashore. In 1881 Manhattan's 22,000 slum tenements held 500,000 people. By 1895 the number of tenements had almost doubled, to 40,000, but the population they contained had risen far higher proportionately—to 1,300,000. And more than 95 percent of those slum dwellers were immigrants and their children.

Living on the Lower East Side meant living in a tenement. New York had divided its building lots into rectangles 25 feet wide by 100 feet long. Twice that space was needed for proper light and air, but profits didn't lie that way. The "dumbbell" tenement became the standard by the time the mass immigration began. Six to seven stories tall, the tenements were arranged in the shape of a dumbbell, four apartments on a floor, two at each end of a narrow separating corridor. The front apartments were usually four rooms; the rear, three. But only one room in each apartment got direct light from the street in front or a yard in the rear. An air shaft less than five feet wide separated

A glimpse into a slum tenement

YIVO Institute for Jewish Research

the tenement buildings. The common toilet was in the hallway.

A reporter took a look at dumbbell tenements on the Lower East Side and summed up his impressions.

They are great prison-like structures of brick, with narrow doors and windows, cramped passages and steep rickety stairs. . . . The narrow courtyard . . . in the middle is a damp foul-smelling place, supposed to do duty as an airshaft; had the foul fiend designed these great barracks they could not have been more villainously arranged to avoid any chance of ventilation. . . . In case of fire they would be perfect death-traps, for it would be impossible for the occupants of the crowded rooms to escape by the narrow stairways, and the flimsy fire escapes which the owners of the tenements were compelled to put up a few years ago are so laden with broken furniture bales and boxes that they would be worse than useless. In the hot summer months . . . these fire-escape balconies are used as sleeping-rooms by the poor wretches who are fortunate enough to have windows opening upon them. The drainage is horrible, and even the Croton as it flows from the tap in the noisome courtyard seemed to be contaminated by its surroundings and have a fetid smell.

Summertime on Orchard Street is recalled by J. R. Schwartz, who reached the East Side in 1899.

There hasn't been any breeze or rain to speak of. The sun beats down mercilessly. The only shade is indoors and indoors it's stifling. People are listless from the energy-sapping heat. The street-cleaner turns on the street hydrant to flush the pavement and let the little kids splash in the gushing stream. The water isn't cold. . . .

You walk along the street. . . . The flies and mosquitoes add to the discomfort. The smells from the uncollected garbage are nauseating. The rivulets in the gutter, sweeping along the slops from the washpail water dumped by the storekeepers, are black and the smells are putrid. Little boys, unabashed, urinate into the flow of bilge and add to the stench.

A pushcart peddler, either too lazy to seek out some toilet or unconcerned about proprieties, urinates against a wagon wheel regardless of the women pedestrians. . . . At another spot you see a middle-aged woman looking for vermin or insects crawling between her breasts while another is sitting in front of a stoop openly suckling her infant. In the middle of the street a wagon stops and the horse lets go a gusher of urine and drops a load of manure.

You look up at the fire escapes and see them filled with the young and the old seeking an elusive breeze. Thinking that here they have privacy, they are clad in flimsy underwear or shirts as token coverages and signs of their modesty.

The worst place in the tenement was a basement or cellar apartment. Lower Manhattan was flat and without enough sewers for the rain and waste to reach the rivers underground. Terrible stinks came up from the street openings and assaulted the basement dwellers. Chicago's slum basements were no better. Lucy Robbins Lang, who came from Russia at nine, remembers hers.

For $4.50 a month Aunt Yente Chave rented rooms for us in the basement of the house on Morgan Street in which she lived, and she also found for us an unsteady table, some lame chairs, a rusty bed, and an ancient sofa.

The basement was divided in two, and we lived in the part toward the street. The front room had a barred window, through which we could see only the feet of passers-by and the rats that thronged under the wooden sidewalk. The second room was the kitchen, and in it was a smoky stove. Then there was a half room, like a cave dug into a black cliff, and the bed was placed there, near the windowless wall. The other half of the basement contained the toilet and the coal bins, which were infested with rats as big as cats. When the tenants came to get coal, they had to fight the rats, which fled towards our apartment. Mother, who was very unwell, lived in fear of the rats.

Privacy in such homes was practically unknown. The average three-room flat had a kitchen, a parlor, and a bedroom. The parlor was converted into sleeping quarters at night, and so was the kitchen when families were large—and they often were. Gussie Kimball recalls that much of social life took place on the other side of the apartment door.

Twenty-four families occupied our tenement, six families on each floor. The halls were very busy places, mostly because the toilets and running water were community services in the halls. If you went to the sink to fetch water, you were bound to meet a neighbor or two. Someone would have a pitcher to fill with drinking water. Someone else would have a cooking pot to fill. And usually a mother would be waiting to fill a tub for her youngsters' baths.

Getting the water was important, but just as important was the chance to talk—or listen. Papa called the halls our "talking newspapers." Here was where the gossip was passed around about who was getting married, or expecting a baby, who was ill or dying, who was having a bris (circumcision), or who was being bar mitzva (confirmed).

"Privacy," said Samuel Chotzinoff, "could be had only in public. The streets in the evening were thick with promenading couples, and the benches around the fountain and in Jackson Street Park, and the empty trucks lined up at the river front were filled with lovers who had no other place to meet."

How the mass of Eastern European Jews felt about living under such conditions we do not know. No scientific surveys of public opinion were made in that time. The nearest we come to it are the impressions set down in autobiographies, stories, poems, plays, and in interviews recorded long after the event.

Writing of a tenement house on Suffolk Street, Leon Kobrin, who immigrated from Russia in 1892, conveys the variety of human life within its walls.

Jewish immigrants live here—most of them working-men and working-women, most of them not working people in the old country . . . on every floor, behind every door, a different past, a separate present, a different life-experience, an isolated existence—one sorrowful, beaten, wounded, hopeless and another cheerful, sunny,

triumphant, filled with hope and expectation. . . . Re-
fined folk and coarse, scholars and ignoramuses, parents
of children who are a source of joy, and of children who
might better not have been born. . . . Children who
had left their parents in the old homes, and yearned for
them, and parents whose American children had de-
serted them. . . . Parents who are ashamed of their off-
spring and children who are ashamed of their parents.
. . . The dreamy eyes of the young, illumined by
thought, and dull eyes of exhausted workers in which
thought has been quenched for a long time. The impu-
dent animalism in the face of a young gangster and the
refined meditative face of a college man—all these are
hidden in the high, gray, stone walls of the tenement
house.

Some felt lost and lonely in the crowded slums. Maurice
Hindus said that he wept with anguish the day he had to
leave the muddy Russian village of his birth.

My ancestors had lived there for centuries, had be-
come intimately intertwined with the life and culture of
our lowly, talkative, hospitable muzhik neighbors. Now I
was leaving it, the only home I had known. Though my
mother, brother, and sisters were with me, I felt the
desolation of the uprooted. Despite poverty, mud, bribe-
extorting Czarist officials, I had loved the old home with
a fierce primitive emotion, and leaving it was like tearing
something out of my very soul.

The tenement flat his family moved into on the Lower
East Side, poor as it was, had many conveniences they had
never known at home. But nothing compensated for what
he had lost.

You couldn't get to love a tenement flat; it was not home. We never stayed long enough in one flat anyway. That was the way it was in the big city. People moved from house to house from one neighborhood to another, never missing the old place, glad perhaps never to have to see it again.

In the big city people were as rootless as tumbleweeds, as flitting as birds. Today's friend might vanish overnight and be gone forever. You felt a sudden void within yourself but there was nothing you could do about it. You were one of a crowd you rubbed shoulders with, strangers about whom you wondered but who vanished as suddenly as they appeared. You yearned for an attachment to something outside of yourself and the yearning remained unsatisfied. You were an alien, belonging nowhere, attached to nothing, alone. Even though you lived with your family, there was no fireside at which to warm the cold inner emptiness.

You lived with your family—and often with many strangers. Samuel Cohen's parents, for instance, had a two-room flat on Bayard Street for which they paid ten dollars a month in rent. They took in four boarders, all dry-goods peddlers, at seventy-five cents a week each, which included morning coffee and his mother's doing their laundry. Yuri Suhl writes of a widow who earned her living by running a "private restaurant" in the kitchen of her flat. She usually had eight or ten boarders crowded around the table, most of them from her own Rumanian village. It was necessary to take in boarders to make ends meet.

The boarder soon became a standard character in Yiddish folklore, the *griner cuzine* of fiction and the stage. In Yiddish humor he figured as the clumsy greenhorn, the fool who tenanted every flat. He suited any fantasy, committing good or evil deeds. But usually, remembers Harry Rosko-lenko, he was "lonely and bereft, a totally alien individual . . . a boarder living with a family in some kind of lack-luster, ego-suffering relationship. He was tolerated, as a rule, merely for the money he paid out. . . ."

The Lower East Side was the beachhead from which many Jews moved further inland. Some were drawn west by friends and others were urged out of New York by immigrant-aid societies who raised the hope of better op-portunities in less crowded places. Everywhere they went the immigrants looked for the cheapest rents in tenements close by a place of work. By the early 1900s the Jews had established a ghetto in Chicago centering on Maxwell Street. Louis Wirth, who taught sociology at the University of Chicago, describes it.

> *Maxwell Street, the ghetto's great outdoor market, is full of color, action, shouts, odors, and dirt. It resembles a medieval European fair more than the market of a great city of today. . . . Buying is an adventure in which one matches his wits against those of an oppo-nent, a Jew. The Jews are versatile; they speak Yiddish among themselves, and Polish, Russian, Lithuanian, Hungarian, Bohemian, and what not, to their customers. They know their tastes and their prejudices. They have on hand ginghams in loud, gay colors for one group, and for one occasion; and drab and black mourning wear for others.*
>
> *The noises of crowing roosters and geese, the cooing of pigeons, the barking of dogs, the twittering of canary birds, the smell of garlic and of cheeses, the aroma of*

onions, apples and oranges, and the shouts and curses of sellers and buyers fill the air. Anything can be bought and sold on Maxwell Street. On one stand, piled high, are odd sizes of shoes long out of style; on another are copper kettles for brewing beer; on a third are second-hand pants; and one merchant even sells odd, broken pieces of spectacles, watches and jewelry, together with pocket knives and household tools salvaged from the collections of junk peddlers.

Everything has value on Maxwell Street, but the price is not fixed. It is the fixing of the price around which turns the whole plot of the drama enacted daily at the perpetual bazaar. . . . The sellers know how to ask ten times the amount that their wares will eventually sell for, and buyers know how to offer a twentieth.

Just as in the Pale of Settlement in the old country, where women did the selling while men studied the Talmud, here many Jewish women had become the best merchants on Maxwell Street.

They almost monopolize the fish, herring, and poultry stands. All the stands are on wheels, and are moved nightly. At five-thirty every morning a mob of men, women and children may be seen flocking into an empty lot . . . where an old man rents pushcarts for twenty-five cents per day. He knows each of his carts individually, and when anyone hastens away with one of his 300-odd vehicles without paying, the owner of the pushcarts comes to the market later and collects. . . . By six o'clock in the morning the best and largest pushcarts have been hauled away. Everyone tries to maneuver for the most favorable position on the street. A corner loca-

tion, especially on Maxwell and Halstead streets, is worth fighting for. Frequently the policeman who patrols the street has to decide who came first and is entitled to squatter rights for the day. After "Charlie the Policeman" has settled all the quarrels, fraternization ensues.

The Jewish immigrants outside New York lived in neighborhoods whose conditions were not much different from those on the Lower East Side. Whether it was Philadelphia, Boston, Baltimore, or a dozen other cities, it was a slum. The housing in Chicago's Jewish ghetto, said Charles Zeublin in 1895, was of the same three types which cursed most Chicago working people.

. . . the small, low, one or two story "pioneer" wooden shanty, erected probably before the street was graded, and hence several feet below the street level; the brick tenement of three or four stories, with insufficient light, bad drainage, no bath, built to obtain the highest possible rent for the smallest possible cubic space; and the third type, the deadly rear tenement, with no light in front, and with the frightful odors of the dirty alley in the rear, too often the workshop of the "sweater" as well as the home of an excessive population. On the narrow pavement of the narrow street in front is found the omnipresent garbage-box, with full measure, pressed down and running over. In all but the severest weather the streets swarm with children, day and night.

7 | Cheese It— the Cops!

Grim as the East Side tenements were, the streets that separated them provided youngsters with soul-satisfying pleasure and perils. Every street had its gang, frowned on by police and parents, but often harmless. The kids talked tough because it was the smart thing to do, and they shot craps in the yards with a lookout stationed for cops. The gangs of the really tough, however, extorted money from weaker boys, stole anything in sight, and fought rival gangs for blood.

The milder kind of gang was formed to play games, especially ball. These had little organization except for a leader who was the strongest or played ball best. Based on a well-defined territory, such gangs detested others on their borders and threw down challenges to combat. Fists, sticks, and stones were the weapons in battles that began after school and broke up around suppertime when family scouts collared the combatants and hurried them home.

In the 1890s asphalt began to replace the stone which had paved the East Side streets. Asphalt was easier to clean and it dried quickly after rain. It made a much better

playing surface than the muddy, slippery, jagged stone. The
new surface was great for marbles, rolling hoops, prisoner's
base, and the variety of ball games developed to suit the
tenement canyons.

One o' cat, a favorite of Jewish boys, was really a form of
baseball, reduced in scale and dispensing with the usual
equipment of bats, balls, gloves, and uniforms. Instead of a
ball, a chunk of wood was whittled to about a four-inch
length and an inch in diameter at the center, tapering to
dull points at each end. There were sides, as in baseball, the
number of players depending on who was around at the
moment. There was no pitcher. The piece of wood was put
on the ground, the batter whacked an end lightly with a
stick, sending the "ball" two or three feet in the air, and
then he struck it as hard as he could with his stick. Sometimes the blow sent it half a block. The batter ran bases
(their number varied) as the fielders tried to grab the
"ball" and make an out by flinging it to a baseman or
tagging the runner. (We played the same game in Worcester, Massachusetts, when I was a child, but we called it
"peggy," our name for the wooden "ball.")

In the summertime there was swimming to enjoy. The
Rutgers Square fountain played all day and boys stripped
and dove into its lowest basin. The law banned it, so one
boy would stand guard over the heap of clothing and holler,
"Cheese it—the cops!" when he spied one coming. The
lookout would grab the clothes and rush off in one direction while the swimmers would jump out of the basin and
scatter in other directions to confuse the cop. They would
meet their sentry at some rendezvous, dress, and stroll away
innocently.

It was no crime to swim in the East River a few blocks

off, so long as you kept your underwear on. But the fountain was better; it was riskier. Still, you didn't really have to play ball or swim or do anything to get fun out of living on the Lower East Side. There was satisfaction in just being an onlooker, as Samuel Chotzinoff said.

There were gang wars to be fought, police to annoy and outwit, and sentimental couples to be teased and ridiculed. Standing unobserved at one's window, one could focus a burning-glass on the face of a person resting on the stone bench of the fountain and relish his annoyance and anger as he tried helplessly to locate his tormentor. From the same vantage point, one could let down a weight attached to a long string, conk the head of a passerby, and draw up the missile before the victim could look around for the offender; or, with the aid of an accomplice stationed on the curb, stretch a string head-high across the sidewalk, which, unseen by some unsuspecting pedestrian, would lift his straw hat or derby from his head and send it rolling down the street. . . . There were ambulances to be run after and horse-cars to hang on to—unobserved by the conductor. If one was on intimate terms with a currier in a livery stable, one could sit bareback astride a horse and ride through the streets.

Something was constantly happening which one had to repair to the spot to see at first hand. People were being knocked down by horse-cars. There were altercations on every street, often ending in blows. The changing of streetcar horses at certain termini was a spectacle well worth a walk of a mile. One could run after an ambulance with a view to being in a position to give an eyewitness account of an accident to one's comrades.

There were parades to be followed, also organ-grinders, bums, and itinerant sellers of cure-alls, who would assemble a crowd in a moment, deliver a stream of seemingly sensible, yet strangely incomprehensible, oratory, quickly dispose of some wares, and suddenly move on. . . .

On election nights, there were bonfires to watch and perhaps assist in making. Fires broke out constantly in all seasons, and the air was seldom free from the clang of fire engines, the shrieks of the siren, and the clatter of the horses on the cobblestones. Following the fire engines could conceivably occupy all one's leisure time. . . .

Diversions were also available closer to home. One could spend a profitable afternoon in one's own back yard. The poles for clotheslines soared five stories in the air. To shinny up a pole was a feat in itself, and the exhilaration felt on reaching the top had a quality of its own. . . . A restaurant in the adjoining house kept its milk cans in our yard. These served for games of leapfrog and also offered a means of revenge on the proprietor of the restaurant, a man insensitive to the need of children to play and make noise. Every time he chased us out of the yard, we would return at night, pry open his milk cans, and drop sand and pebbles in them. . . .

Tenement roofs offered a series of connected playgrounds. The element of danger in playing tag on roofs was considerable enough to heighten the ordinary excitement of the game. Cornices were only knee-high. They could hardly be a barrier to destruction should one, in running to escape the tagger, fail to have the presence of mind to veer quickly to right or left. Some buildings were taller than others, this necessitating a thrilling drop of ten or twelve feet, and on returning, an equally excit-

ing scrambling up skylights and chimneys. A breath-taking hazard was the open air shafts that separated houses otherwise contiguous. To miss, even by an inch, a jump over an airshaft meant death, but death did not really matter. For death was only an academic concept, a word without reality, at worst something that could happen only to others.

Evenings the candy store became the social center. It served as an informal clubhouse where schoolchildren could meet old friends and make new ones. In 1900 a *Tribune* reporter counted at least fifty in the Tenth Ward, all of which had a young clientele. Some were used as meeting places for clubs. The newsman described the typical candy store.

A counter along the length of the store decked with cheap candles and perhaps with cigar and cigarette boxes, and invariably a soda water fountain make up the entire furniture of the store, if we except a few cigarette pictures on the wall. Usually the proprietor lives with his family in the rear of the store. Some stores, making a pretense of stylishness, have partitioned off a little room from the store to which they give the elegant name of "ice cream parlor," a sign over the door apprising you of its existence. One or two bare tables and a few chairs furnish the "ice cream parlor." But this little room is very useful as a meeting place for a small club for boys or as a general lounging room. Occasionally a dozen or more youngsters are entertained here by a team of aspiring amateur comedians of the ages of sixteen or seventeen, whose sole ambition is to shine on the stage of some Bowery theater. The comedian or comedians will try their new "hits" on their critical audiences (and a more critical one cannot be found), dance, jig, and tell the jokes heard by them in the continuous performances at vaudeville theaters.

Of course, the candy-store owner didn't welcome the boys out of the goodness of his heart. He charged them a small fee if they borrowed his playing cards, and if they played for money, as they usually did, he took his cut. He took his chances too, for he had to guard against vandalism and thievery.

Was it all fun? And what about the girls? Lincoln Steffens, who covered the Jewish quarter in the 1890s, observed how quickly children, especially the girls, took on the burdens of adults.

The children, acquiring English quickly, with the adaptability of tender years, often assume the responsibilities that would rightfully belong to their elders. One girl of eleven habitually signs the checks and does all the writing necessary in transactions with certain charitable bureaus that help her mother, and during her mother's illness undertook the cooking, washing, and general superintendence of five younger children, one of whom was an infant. When the baby had croup she doctored him herself, and on another occasion kept a paid position for her mother, proving an admirable substitute until she could be relieved. . . .

Another little girl is the real, although her mother is the ostensible janitress of a big tenement house, the child conducting all the interviews with Board of Health officials, the streetcleaners and other authorities, and personally conducting interviews regarding the renting of rooms, collecting, etc. She undertakes to make her bay-lodgers behave well and to enforce proper attention to the contracted area dignified by the term of "yard," generally coming off victor in the pitched battles in which she has to engage.

8 | Peddlers and Pushcarts

"The Jewish needle," said reporter Jacob Riis in 1890, "made America the best-dressed nation in the world." It also came close to enslaving the immigrant generation in the sweatshops where that needle was plied. A majority of the newcomers entered the garment industry, but they could be found in many other trades, for none was barred to them. A report of their occupations made in 1910 showed a rich variety. They were not only in clothing but in the building trades, they were cabinetmakers, tinsmiths and house painters, metalworkers and mechanics, blacksmiths and plumbers, tobacco workers and watchmakers, roofers, masons, locksmiths, electricians, furriers, jewelers, leatherworkers, bookbinders, printers. . . .

In the old country, the proletarian occupations—work you did with your hands—had been looked down upon. The unschooled people, the laborers and artisans who did the dirty work, these were the *prosteh*, the lower class of Jews. They were the great mass of Jews in Eastern Europe. A small minority of Jews did not work with their hands, but lived by trading on some scale—merchants, dealers, shopkeepers. These were the *sheyneh*, the fine Jews. It was more respectable to be your own boss, even in a losing enterprise, than to work for someone else. Part of the distinction between the *sheyneh* and the *prosteh* had to do with using your head. To make your living with your brains rather than your brawn was somehow better. It meant therefore that the more learned too (whether they earned anything or not), such as rabbi, teacher, cantor, or student, fell into the superior class.

America upset the old distinctions. Here it was no disgrace to work with your hands. Workers were not held in contempt. A carpenter or a house painter was as good an American as anyone else. The immigrant Jews soon found that to have your son become a rabbi no longer brought prestige. Instead, parents pointed their sons to the secular professions—medicine, law, pharmacy, dentistry.

As for women, only the lower class (but they were by far the majority) worked in the old country. Before marriage, they might be domestics or seamstresses. After marriage, if the husband devoted himself to the study of the Talmud, the wife became the breadwinner. Women ran shops, kept stalls in the marketplace, baked knishes and rolls at home or baked matzos in factories, raised vegetables, tended cattle, labored endlessly at anything that would keep the family going.

In America, Jewish parents tried to keep their daughters out of the factories. Better to have them stay in public school, if they could get by without their wages, and then send them on to a business course so that they could get jobs as office workers. The girl who was able to become a bookkeeper or a teacher had reached the top of the ladder.

The bottom of the ladder for many immigrants was

peddling. It was the simplest way to enter the world of commerce. In the old country, Jews in the *shtetl* had made goods available to the peasants in the countryside. Here the peddler found his first market among other immigrants. They were poor, they would rather trade with people like themselves, they could not afford the new and the best, they were willing to use the secondhand, the castoffs, the misfits.

The peddler's store was his pack. It took little capital to start, only the will to work hard for small profit. Arriving in the 1880s, Samuel H. Cohen began peddling tinware utensils. They were widely used in the tenements—pails, dishpans, cups, plates, wash boilers, baby rattles. The smaller articles you stowed in a big basket, slung by a strap on your back. In front, hanging by another strap, you carried a wash boiler filled with miscellaneous dishpans and other articles the basket couldn't hold. When fully loaded, only your head and arms could be seen.

On Sam's first day out—he was going on sixteen—the tinware dealer helped him pack front and rear expertly, and told him what block across the Bowery to start working.

At my first port of call my heart was in my mouth. I hesitated. Taking a long breath I climbed up a stoop and yanked the bell. I was in suspense. The door opened. A red-headed young giant appeared. He looked at me and my outfit without a word. He was not a bit rough. He merely laid his hand very gently on the boiler in front of me and gave me a good shove. I descended backwards rapidly, finally landing in a sitting position in the middle of the street, my stock strewn about me in all directions. With great effort I managed to readjust my basket and wash boiler. Now what? I thought I couldn't pull an-

other bell if I tried. I turned back to Elizabeth Street.
Entering a yard I saw an open door—a woman near it. I
made my first sale—a cup for ten cents—the profit was
not bad! It was now near noontime. I saw girls eating on
the first floor near the window. One of them motioned
that I come nearer. I did. I was soon pelted with all the
egg pancake they had left.

He went back to the dealer, dropped his load, and
quit.

Early the next morning he tried selling fans—it was hot
weather—and by nine at night had made five dollars. Then
it turned cool. No sales. For one week he huckstered hair-
pins. Matches were next; they were needed to start the
kerosene lamps.

With several packs in a bag, some loose packages in
my hand, I started out. It was a case of running up and
down stairways the whole day long. I kept a record of a
day's work. I climbed the stairs of fifty houses, with an
average of four flights to each. It made two hundred
flights of stairs per day. Sales averaged about $2. Net
profit was seventy-five cents.

But up and down two hundred flights of stairs daily was
too much for him to endure. For a while he peddled dust-
ers and whisk brooms office to office in the financial district. That didn't produce enough to live on either. He
quit, this time for good.

Many came to the same dead end. Others did better.
While the economy was expanding, they made their way
from pack or pushcart to chromium and plate-glass store.
And some to department-store baronies. If you weren't

Pushcarts on Hester Street in 1898

tough enough, you caved in fast. Nathan Kuskin bought $1.47 worth of cotton, pins, shoelaces, matches, and other notions, put them in a basket, then walked past block after block of Philadelphia's houses, trying to get up enough nerve to ring the first doorbell. When at last he rang a bell, a woman came to the door. He stood there dumbly: he didn't know the right English words to offer his wares. He uncovered his basket, and the woman took a package of pins and gave him a nickel. He thanked her and walked away. He knew she didn't need the pins. She had given him the money as charity. He was through. No push, no nerve, no success, not in this trade.

The West, where other greenhorns had gone before you, might be a greener pasture. Bernard Horwich described the peddlers he saw on the West Side of Chicago, a filthy place where crime was rampant and Jews were beaten on the streets. Most peddlers went from house to house, carrying packs of notions and light dry goods, or junk and vegetables. Every streetcar bore Jewish peddlers riding to and from their routes. While many peddlers had no other trade, some were skilled workers who were obliged in dull seasons to do anything because work in the busy season had not paid enough to carry the family over. They took up basket or pushcart to bring in a few pennies.

The pushcarts sold a fantastic variety of merchandise. "It ran," according to J. R. Schwartz's alliterative threnody, "from knishes to knick-knacks, from vegetables to vests, from lamps to leeks, and from pickles to pants." There were even peddlers selling packages of dirt, the genuine mother earth from Jerusalem. If you paid a peddler's asking price, you were considered an easy mark. A good shopper mastered the fine art of haggling. Schwartz, who was a medical student in 1910, was told to buy Weisse's *Dissection of the Human Body*. Its price was $6.50. He didn't have the money, and had to share a classmate's copy. One day, strolling along the seven blocks of stores and pushcarts that made up Orchard Street, he came across a cart piled high with books. And there was a copy of Weisse! His heart skipped a beat.

I looked at the vendor, an elderly Jew, and wondered how much he knew about the books he was selling. Without displaying any interest or enthusiasm I casually asked him what he wanted for this book. He took it from me, looked it over in a sort of knowing manner, hefted it for weight and said:

"Far dem buch vill ich haben finif und sibetzik cent." (*For this book I want seventy-five cents.*)

I put on a look of indifference and told him I thought it was too much money.

"Aber zey nor, zindele, es hat a sach bilder." (*But look, sonny, it has a lot of pictures.*)

I offered him twenty-five cents. He looked at me with compassion and said, "Wie azoi ken ich machen a leben as ich beit bei dir finif und sibetzik cent und die gibst mir nor finif und tzwantzik. Nu, freg ich dich, is das a geschaft?" (*How can I make a living when I ask you seventy-five cents and you offer me only twenty-five cents? Is this a business?*)

But right away he came down to sixty cents. I offered him thirty and he came down to fifty, with the final upshot that I got it for forty cents.

There were peddlers who sold the sacred as well as the profane. In Boston, E. E. Lisitzky's father peddled rags and bottles during the day and in the evening peddled Hebrew lessons to Jewish boys preparing for Bar Mitzvah. During the month between Purim and Passover he also walked the streets selling Passover necessities (matzo, wine, etc.) on the installment plan. The son's memory of the way his father eked out a livelihood conveys the miseries of peddling.

Every morning, after the services and breakfast, he would stick on his hat a brass badge marked with black letters and numbers against a glossy background—the badge which the Boston authorities had ordered every rag peddler to wear—shoulder his sack, and leave for work. He walked his route through the city, crying "R-r-rags and bot-tles!" He looked up at the tenement houses, looking at the windows for a sign that one of the tenants wanted to bargain over their discards and rags. Sometimes young rowdies threw stones at him, and in the winter snowballs with pieces of coal inside, sometimes hoodlums pulled his beard, sometimes he'd be attacked in dark hallways and his pockets emptied. "Rags and bottles!" he would call again after such a mishap, his voice ringing with pain and grief, but not with bitterness or protest. He was inured to suffering and submitted to it.

The boys he peddled Bar Mitzvah lessons to much preferred playing ball to reading in the Hebrew prayer book. The lessons were forced upon them by their parents; the boys made life hard for the man who sold them pieces of his learning for pennies.

His customers lived far apart, but the pennies he earned through so much toil were too precious to be spent on streetcar travel, so he half-ran, half-walked from lesson to lesson. Late at night he dragged his weary feet home. After prayers he sat down to an appetiteless supper—work had killed his hunger.

Orchard Street lured crowds not only from the surrounding East Side but from far-off Brooklyn and the Bronx. The bargains were said to be the best in America, so why not? Everything was for sale cheap and in a hurry because there was no place to store unsold goods. If you bought in the stores lining Orchard Street, you were sure to pay more. It was the pushcarts (1,500 of them, one newspaper estimated) which offered the best bargains. The peddlers paid twenty-five dollars a year for their licenses and rented their carts for a dime a day.

Harry Roskolenko was raised near Orchard Street's universal market and never forgot what he saw.

The pushcarts came small, came large, came bigger than large—and in double or triple tiers. . . . These conglomerate street bargains had a variety of prices—depending on the age, the smell, the look, and certainly the taste, for you were offered a taste of everything edible and not edible. Milk sold for two cents a quart, with your own pitcher. It was ladled out of 40-quart cans that were not too clean. It was done in a splash by the husband or the wife, depending on who was nearest to the huge milk cans. . . . Butter, smelling a bit rancid, sold for five cents a pound—smell and all. Bread, a cent a pound; but if you wanted a half of a pound it was cut for you from a huge round bread weighing over twenty pounds.

Potatoes, sacked, were bought to make the winter viable. Nobody bothered to buy a pound of potatoes.

Potatoes came in sacks weighing fifty pounds—and off we went, father and sons, carrying the sack ten blocks to home. Prunes, plums, tangerines—all of our fruits— came in round crates, and similarly were hauled off home. The difference between prices when buying in bulk and buying in small amounts was something that made bankers of all of us on Orchard Street—the earliest street of bulk and container packaging done in a hurry. As for grapefruits, nobody trusted them yet. They were a bastard fruit, as tomatoes once had been. My mother called tomatoes "love apples"—whatever that must have meant to her. I thought tomatoes were invented to throw at the rich or the street-corner politicians around Election Day.

Making cigars and cigarettes was a trade which many immigrants entered in those early years before mass production of tobacco products. Two of Sam Chotzinoff's sisters made cigarettes in their Lower East Side home. Their combined weekly piecework earnings ran to four or five dollars. At the age of ten, Lucy Robbins Lang went to work as a tobacco stripper in a cigar shop in Chicago. Because the owners had known her grandfather in Kiev, they paid the beginner a dollar a week; most children were paid nothing while learning the trade and some even paid tuition for the privilege. Lucy worked from 7 A.M. to 6 P.M., and since carfare would have eaten up her weekly dollar, she walked to work, an hour each way. Maurice Sterne's first job in New York was like Lucy's: at eleven he stripped tobacco in the rear of a cigar store on Eighth Avenue.

To learn many of the trades you had to pay a sizable fee, twenty-five to fifty dollars, and work at least one to three months for nothing. Unable to raise that amount, Samuel Cohen went into a cigarette factory on Water Street in New York. The hours were as long as Lucy's in Chicago, the tobacco stuck in your throat and nose, but, he was told, the labor wasn't as killing as in the garment trade: "You just use your fingers." The process seemed intricate and difficult to the beginner, but he saw other workers could roll 500 cigarettes in one hour. Sam's first week's earnings were $2.42. The second week he made 4,000 cigarettes, at eighty cents per thousand, less shortages and poor work, and received $3.10 in his pay envelope. "It was a thrill," he said. "I could almost eat."

In this cradle song by the poet Morris Rosenfeld, a sweatshop worker laments that his inhumanly long hours never permit him to see his baby awake.

LULLABY

Ich hob a kley-nem yin-ge-le, A zu-ne-le gor fayn. Ven ich der-ze im dacht zich mir: Di gant-se velt iz mayn. Nor zelt-n, zelt-n ze ich im, Mayn shey-nem ven er vacht. Ich tref im im-er shlofn-dig, Ich ze im nor bay-nacht.

Ich hob a kleynem yingele,
A zunele gor fayn.
Ven ich derze im, dacht zich mir:
Di gantse velt iz mayn.

Nor zeltn, zeltn, ze ich im,
Mayn sheynem ven er vacht.
Ich tref im imer shlofndig,
Ich ze im nor baynacht.

Di arbet traybt mich fri aroys,
Un lozt mich shpet tsurik.
O, fremd iz mir mayn eygn layb,
O, fremd mayn kind's a blik.

I have a little boy,
A little son so fine.
And when I look at him I think:
The whole world is mine.

But seldom, seldom, do I see him,
My lovely one, awake.
I always find him sleeping,
I see him only at night.

My toil drives me out early,
And brings me home so late.
O, strange to me is my own flesh
And strange my own child's
glance.

9 | Sweatshop

If the immigrant didn't turn to peddling as the way to make a living in "the golden country," the chances are he found work in the clothing industry. Either one meant hard work for low pay. The clothing shops were usually overcrowded, dirty, badly lit, poorly ventilated rooms where men, women, and children labored in a speed-up system for fifteen or even eighteen hours a day. At least 60 percent of the newcomers entered the needle trades. Many had never done manual labor in the old country, where they might have been yeshiva students, teachers, clerks, insurance agents, bookkeepers, storekeepers. Here they were harnessed to machines which hurried them to the last breath.

The documents of those days contain few happy accounts of life in the garment trades. They are full of frustration and anger. One immigrant wrote, "There was no one who liked his work. All hated it and all sought a way of being free of it. All looked upon the boss as upon their enemy, the exploiter who fattens upon the marrow of his workers and gets rich on their account." The disappointments they met made them curse Columbus for having discovered the country. (A *klog tzu Columbus!*)

The garment industry was expanding rapidly in the late nineteenth century. And like earlier immigrants of whatever nationality, the Jews turned to wherever the work was. It had nothing to do with a talent for the needle or previous training. (Only about 10 percent had been tailors in Europe.) Here was an industry clamoring for cheap labor and here was a mass of people who had to take any kind of work to stay alive. Most of the early garment makers were German Jews. In Germany, Jews had often dealt in new and secondhand clothing. Arriving here in midcentury, they began as peddlers or retail merchants and moved up to manufacturing. By 1880 there were over 500 shops employing 25,000 workers. As the immigration tide rolled in, the German Jews gave work to large numbers of the newcomers. The sewing machine, the cutting knife, the shears and flatiron became the tools by which thousands earned their living in Chicago, Boston, Philadelphia, Baltimore. And most of all in New York, the heart of the needle trades. By 1890, some 13,000 Jews were on the great East Side treadmill. Ten years later, over 150,000 Jewish immigrants and their families were making their living in the garment industry.

The development of the sewing machine made it possible. It revolutionized the production of clothing of all kinds. Before its invention, tailor-made suits and dresses, cut and fitted by skilled craftsmen, could be afforded only by the rich. Now immigrant workers could be swiftly taught the modest skills needed to operate machines that could mass-produce ready-made clothing from standard patterns. Long and costly apprenticeships were no longer necessary. Each step of production was broken down into smaller and simpler processes. What was demanded of the

YIVO Institute for Jewish Research

Boss and workers pose for the photographer in a shirt and blouse shop on the Lower East Side

worker was speed, dexterity, and willingness to submit to the endless round of dull and repetitive tasks. This piece-work system brought new and fashionable clothing within the reach of the millions for the first time.

But it was done at great cost to the garment worker. The production system which rapidly came to dominate the industry trapped men, women, and children in the infamous "sweatshop." Bernard Weinstein describes one.

> *The boss of the shop lived there with his entire family. The front room and kitchen were used as workrooms. The whole family would sleep in one dark bedroom. The sewing-machines for the operators were located near the windows of the front room. The basters would sit on stools near the walls, and in the center of the room, midst the dirt and the dust, were heaped great piles of materials. There, on top of the soft piles, several finishers would be sitting. . . . Old people . . . using gaslight for illumination, would stand and keep the irons hot and press the finished coats, jackets, pants and other clothes on special boards.*

Baxter Street on the Lower East Side housed many sweatshop workers. There was nothing romantic or noble about the way they lived. Outsiders coming down to look for local color found only dark and ugly tones. One visitor, Edward W. Townsend, sketched his realistic impression of Baxter Street in 1895.

> *The people, from the youngest to the oldest, were speechless and grave and hopeless-looking. Men staggered past, their bodies bent almost double under what seemed impossible loads of clothing they were carrying*

*to and from the sweaters' and the workshop-homes;
women carrying similar bundles on their heads, or perhaps a bundle of wood from some builder's waste, not
speaking to those they passed; none of the children seen
was much more than a baby in years, and they were
silent, too, and had no games: they were in the street
because while the sweaters' work went on there was no
room for them in their homes. In the dress of none was
any bright color, and the only sounds were the occasional
cry of a hurt child, the snarling of the low-browed men
who solicited trade for the clothing stores, quarrelling for
the possession of a chance victim; and always, as the
grinding ocean surf mutters an accompaniment to all
other shore sounds—always, always, always—was heard
the whirring monotone of the sewing-machine.*

Tenement-house manufacture spread rapidly in Chicago
too, entering many industries besides the garment trade.
Wherever the system went, the trade became a sweated
one, carried on in the worst conditions. Only full exposure
of the harsh facts of human suffering could hope to effect
change. Florence Kelley described in a state-sponsored report the Chicago garment sweatshops which investigators
visited in 1894.

*Shops over sheds or stables, in basements or on upper
floors of tenement houses, are not fit working places for
men, women, and children.*

*Most of the places designated in this report as base-
ments are low-ceiled, ill-lighted, unventilated rooms, below the street level; damp and cold in winter, hot and
close in summer; foul at all times by reason of adjacent
vaults or defective sewer connections. The term cellar*

would more accurately describe these shops. Their dampness entails rheumatism and their darkness injures the sight of the people who work in them. They never afford proper accommodation for the pressers, the fumes of whose gasoline stoves and charcoal heaters mingle with the mouldy smell of the walls and the stuffiness always found where a number of the very poor are crowded together.

In shops over sheds or stables the operatives receive from below the stench from the vaults or the accumulated stable refuse; from the rear, the effluvia of the garbage boxes and manure bins in the filthy, unpaved alleys; and from the front, the varied stenches of the tenement house yard, the dumping ground for all the families residing on the premises.

Shops on upper floors have no proper ventilation; are reached by narrow and filthy halls and unlighted wooden stairways; are cold in winter unless all fresh air is shut out, and hot in summer. If in old houses, they afford no sanitary arrangements beyond the vaults used by all tenants; if in modern tenements the drains are out of order, water for the closets does not rise to upper floors, and poisonous gases fill the shops. This defective water supply, the absence of fire escapes and the presence of the pressers' stove greatly aggravate the danger of death by fire.

Shops on the middle floors are ill-lighted, ill-ventilated, and share the smells from the kitchens and drains of surrounding living rooms.

As "greeners" came off the boat, their relatives already here steered them into the sweatshops. Or the newly arrived immigrant would go to the "Pig Market," a sort of labor exchange which grew up around Hester and Essex streets. There he would stand and wait for a contractor in need of "green hands" to offer him a job. Both workers and employers often came from the same towns in Eastern Europe. One *landsmann* hired another or taught another. S. L. Blumenson recalls the early 1900s when about 80 percent of the bosses and workers in the section of the industry which made children's coats (called "reefers") were *landsleit* or relatives.

> *They all came from a small district in Lithuania, the* uyezd *or county of Hooman, in the province of Minsk— from such villages as Schmilovits, Dukor, Puchovitch, Hooman, Bobroisk, Berezin. . . .*
>
> *Most of the manufacturers were graduates of a pio- neer shop established in a loft on alley-like Pelham Street, near Pike. . . . This shop was opened in the year 1889 by an immigrant from Dukor, his two sons, and his son-in-law. The father was a tailor by trade, as was the son-in-law. The two sons, however, were ex-yeshiva* bochurim, *and excellent Hebrew scholars. When they opened their own shop, after working in various sweat- shops, the father did the cutting and finishing and press- ing, and the other three operated the sewing machines. The business grew and prospered, and it soon became a beehive of new immigrants from the county of Hooman. Older men, small town* baalabaatim (*householders*), *be- came pressers; younger men became* araushelfers (*help- ers to operators*), *and the young women, mostly teenage, became finishers.*

In one of his stories Sholem Asch depicts such a *lands- mann* operation on the East Side, where a whole village from the old country became faithful slaves to the "pharaoh" of the sweatshop, Uncle Moses.

> *Kuzmin sat at work, sewing coats, trousers and vests for persons whom they would never see. The whole village of Kuzmin worked upstairs in Uncle Moses' shop. There was Reb Joel Chayim, the head of the synagogue, and Itshe the cobbler's boy, and Junder the ladies' tailor—the dandy of Kuzmin, who once had woven a spell around the hearts of Kuzmin's beauties. . . . All Kuzmin sat there sewing for Uncle Moses; he had reduced the entire population to the same level. There were no more leading citizens, synagogue dignitaries and humble artisans—no more Talmudic experts and coarse fellows. No more cobblers, foremen, men who applied bleeding-cups to women . . . and men who tickled the women while they fitted on their dresses. All now served a single idol; all performed the same rite—they sewed trousers.*

To be part of that substantially segregated economy was like being part of the *shtetl*. Jews worked for Jews and the relations between them (often bitter class conflict) were carried on within the framework of a ghetto. Yiddish, the mother tongue, was everyone's language, boss or worker. The Jewish immigrant who entered such an environment immediately on arrival might have no need for the English language so long as he stayed within this small world.

The fact that Jewish workers labored for Jewish bosses created a unique situation other ethnic groups did not share. The non-Jewish immigrant's job was rarely inside his own ethnic neighborhood. He never encountered the owner of the mine or mill or railroad where he worked. His foreman probably spoke only English. The mark of the worker's foreignness brought down upon him derision and contempt. But Jewish workers and employers shared roots, religion, culture, history. Which was why in the beginning, and for some time after, Jewish workers organized into Jewish unions.

The garment industry became the typical trade of the tenements. No other in the city or state of New York employed so many workers. The thousands of shops jammed into the streets below Fourteenth produced over half of America's ready-made clothing. It grew so fast because of the enormous demand both here and abroad for its products. But also because the unit of industrial production was small. What better chance was there to set up your own shop, and move up from worker to boss? S. L. Blumenson shows how the reefer makers from Hooman did it.

In time, some . . . opened places of their own, two or three pooling their skills and their few dollars. It did not require much capital to start a small factory. A dark hole of a loft, more often than not over a smelly stable, at a monthly rental of ten or twelve dollars, a few wooden horses and boards for a cutting table, a few chairs, a long cutting knife, and a gas or wood stove for the solid press irons—these made up a shop. Every operator had to supply his own sewing machine.

The "capitalists" bought a few bolts of very cheap cloth, cheap even for those days, and manufactured children's wearing apparel ranging in price from 90 cents to $2 a piece wholesale, and women's and misses' finery from $1.50 to $3.75. Despite these low prices, and to compensate for the cheapness of the cloth, these gar-

ments had to have "style." Yards and yards of soutache, braid, and gimp were sewed onto them in all manner of geometric design, and some were trimmed with innumerable ornamental buttons. It does not require a cost accountant to determine that little was left over for the payroll.

And that little the boss whittled down to even less by a system of extortionate fines. If a worker was late five minutes, half a day's pay forfeit. If he left work too early, half a day's pay more. If he fainted from the heat on the job, a day's pay lost. If he didn't return an empty spool, fifty cents fine; if he lost a "number" ticket, twenty-five cents fine.

The Yiddish labor poet Morris Rosenfeld, who sweated in a garment factory, cried out against the cost to the human spirit:

> The Clock in the workshop—it rests not a moment;
> It points on, and ticks on: eternity—time;
> Once someone told me the clock had a meaning,—
> In pointing and ticking had reason and rhyme . . .
> At times, when I listen, I hear the clock plainly;—
> The reason of old—the old meaning—is gone!
> The maddening pendulum urges me forward
> To labor and still labor on.
> The tick of the clock is the boss in his anger.
> The face of the clock has the eyes of the foe.
> The clock—I shudder—Dost hear how it draws me?
> It calls me "Machine" and it cries [to] me "Sew!"

Sam Liptzin tells of bosses he worked under who were like Haman, that tyrant of tyrants. An especially bad one was Levy & Son on Chrystie Street.

There was no clock in the shop. Wages were paid every three or four weeks and even then, in "part payments." Worst of all, however, was the sadistic nature of Mr. Levy. He once caught an operator smoking at a machine. He crept up in back of the man, snatched the cigarette out of his hand and choked it out against his arm. In the washroom he removed the door from the stall, to prevent anyone smoking there or taking a few moments' rest.

Another boss named Strickman liked to pull "practical jokes."

One of the workers, Lazer the finisher, had been complaining that the thread was rotten and falling apart in his hands. Strickman pretended to stage an experiment to test the strength of the thread. He pulled and pulled on a length of thread until it broke and his fist struck Lazer, standing nearby, in the eye. Lazer's vision was irreparably damaged by this "accidental" blow. But this was not enough for Mr. Strickman. He made up a "clever joke." Afterward, whenever Lazer had trouble threading a needle, he would say, "Here, Lazer, take this chalk and put a mark on the needle, so you'll know where the hole is!"

In the sweatshop system manufacturers distributed material to contractors. They in turn subcontracted it to people who did the tasks in their homes. The system began here early in the nineteenth century, when immigrant English tailors and then Irish tailors brought into their homes the work handed out by the contractors.

When the sewing machine arrived and introduced divi-

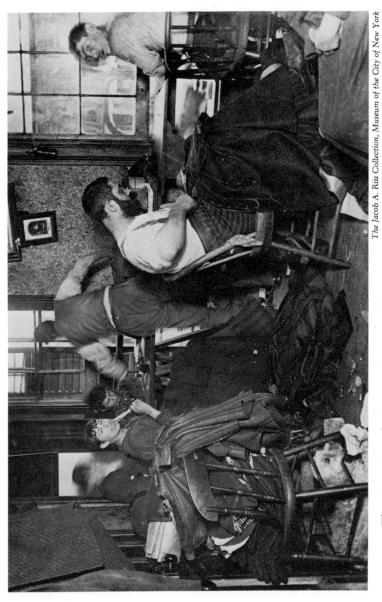

The pioneering photo-journalist Jacob Riis invaded the tenements with a newly invented flash powder that illuminated the dark side of East Side life. Some of these workers in a Ludlow Street sweatshop moved just as the flash ignited

sion of labor, the older tailors, reluctant to adopt the new methods, were replaced by the Jewish immigrants. Around 1900 the "sweating district"—bounded by Eighth Street, the Bowery, Catherine Street, and the East River—enclosed some 450,000 people living and working in the tenements. The most intense competition was fostered by the sweating system. Competing manufacturers farmed out the material for garments to competing contractors, who in turn distributed it to men and women competing for the work of making up the garments. There were usually several stages in the process. Wholesale manufacturers cut and bunched garments, distributing them in job lots to smaller contractors. Each of these specialized, one taking coats, another trousers, still another dresses, and so on. These smaller shops might do some of the work in their own place, and subdivide the rest among the "sweaters"—men who operated in their own tenement homes. The sweater's family lived in one of the few rooms, the others occupied by ten or twenty sewers and pressers employed by him. But he too might subcontract some of the work given him, handing the material on to other families in the neighborhood who would make up the finished garments and deliver them to him. At each step downward profit was sweated out of the next in line, with the tiniest compensation left for the super-exploited worker at the bottom.

The contractor was more than a mere middleman. He had to know tailoring in order to organize the labor called for. The tasks were broken down into various grades and forms of skill—baster, machinist, presser, and then their subdivisions, such as fitter, busheler, finisher, buttonhole maker, feller, bagging puller, and so on. The economist John R. Commons discussed the attributes of a contractor or sweater in a 1901 report of the U.S. Industrial Commission.

The man best fitted to be a contractor is the man who is well acquainted with his neighbors, who is able to speak the language of several classes of immigrants, who can easily persuade his neighbors or their wives and children to work for him, and in this way can obtain the cheapest help. The contractor can increase the number of people employed in the trade at very short notice. During the busy season, when the work doubles, the number of people employed increases in the same proportion. All of the contractors are agents and go around among the people. Housewives, who formerly worked at the trade and abandoned it after marriage, are called into service for an increased price of a dollar or two a week. Men who have engaged in other occupations, such as small business, peddling, etc., and are out of the business most of the year, are marshaled into service by the contractor, who knows all of them, and can easily look them up and put them in as competitors, by offering them a dollar or two a week more than they are getting elsewhere.

The sweating system prolonged a primitive mode of production. Power for the sewing machines came from the foot, and the shops were in homes, alleys, attics, over stables. Low rent and low wages enabled small shops to compete successfully with the large factories powered by steam or electricity. Ironically, a relatively liberal labor law (compared with earlier conditions) in New York State gave sweaters a competitive edge. The law limited working hours to ten per day, required a forty-five-minute lunch break, a closing time of 9 P.M., and curbed child labor. But the law applied only to work done in the factory. The *home*—that was different, a man's private affair. So the home sweatshops could recruit immigrant workers fresh from the old country and pay them piece rates so low they had to work fifteen to eighteen hours a day, and often seven days a week, for enough to stay alive.

An outsider's view of the sweatshop comes from Ernest Poole, the novelist. In 1903 he went down into the Lower East Side on a magazine assignment. He wanted to see how the small coat shops were operated. It was nine at night, and the lights were burning everywhere.

> *The room is low and crowded. The air is close, impure, and alive with the ceaseless whir of machines. The operator bends close over his machine—his foot on the treadle in swift, ceaseless motion; the baster stands just behind, at the table; the finisher works close between them. On the table is a pile of twenty coats. This is their "task"—the day's work, which most teams never accomplish. Of the three teams here, the swiftest can finish their task in fourteen hours' labor. The other two seem forever behind and striving to catch up. Five tasks a week is their average. They need no overseer, no rules, no regular hours. They drive themselves. This is the secret of the system, for three men seldom feel sick or dull or exhausted at the same moment. If the operator slackens his pace, the baster calls for more coats. If at six o'clock the baster gives out, the finisher spurs him on through the evening.*
>
> *The positions are tense, their eyes strained, their movements quick and nervous. Most of them smoke*

cigarettes while they work; beer and cheap whiskey are brought in several times a day by a peddler. Some sing Yiddish songs—while they race. The women chat and laugh sometimes—while they race. For these are not yet dumb slaves, but intensely human beings—young, and straining every nerve of youth's vitality. Among operators twenty years is an active lifetime. Forty-five is old age. They make but half a living.

By this time the small shops had lost much ground to the large factories. About 70 percent of the coats, for instance, were now factory-made. How did it happen? And was it better for the worker? Ernest Poole answers:

Endless saving, dividing, narrowing labor—this is the factory. Down either side of the long factory table forty operators bend over machines, and each one sews the twentieth part of a coat. One man makes hundreds of pockets. On sewing pockets his whole working life is narrowed. To this intensity he is helped and forced and stimulated at every possible point. His strength is no longer wasted on pushing a treadle; the machine is run by power. The coat passes down the long bench, then through the hands of a dozen pressers and basters and finishers—each doing one minute part swiftly, with exact precision. Through thirty hands it comes out at last fourteen minutes quicker, four cents cheaper; the factory has beaten the task shop.

And the human cost—is it, too, reduced? Is the worker better off here than he was in the sweatshop? To consider this fairly we must compare the nonunion factory with the nonunion sweatshop. Wages by the week for the most skilled workers are slightly higher in the factory than they were in the sweatshop. They are lower for the unskilled majority. This majority must slowly increase, for the factory system progresses by transferring skill to machinery. Hours are shorter; work is less irregular; the shop is sanitary; the air is more wholesome—but the pocket maker is often as exhausted at 6 P.M. as the coat maker was at 10 P.M., for his work is more minute, more intense, more monotonous. This concentration, too, is growing.

10 | Where Children Slowly Roast

The pleasures and opportunities of childhood were denied to millions of immigrant boys and girls who supplied cheap and unskilled labor to the employers. If adults were exploited unfeelingly, the lot of children was even worse. Some sewed coats in sweatshops, some made paper lanterns, artificial flowers, paper boxes, some sold papers, shined shoes, minded pushcarts, some labored in printing plants or woodyards or ran messages for the telegraph company.

A physician who treated people on the Lower East Side said that wherever she found working children their wages made up the greater part of the family income. An example was a woman whose husband was under treatment for tuberculosis. The wife went out to do washing whenever she could get the work. Their three children, eleven, seven, and five, worked at home covering wooden buttons with silk at four cents for every twelve dozen. The oldest went to school, but worked with the others evenings and weekends. The family's combined wages were three to six dollars per week, with children earning two thirds of it.

Child labor was nothing new, of course. As early as 1832, two out of five workers in the factories of New England were children under sixteen. Employers preached that idleness was bad for children. In 1870 over 700,000 children aged ten to fifteen were at work. In 1880 the number had risen to over 1,000,000, and in 1900 to 1,750,000. Nearly one of every five children in the country was working for wages.

Maurice Sterne, as an immigrant boy of twelve, went to work in a flag factory on the Lower West Side of New York. The year was 1892; Grover Cleveland was running for President and there was a big demand for small flags to carry in election parades.

The factory was on the third floor of a four-story loft building. The only light came from gas jets burning overhead, the heat in summer was stifling, and there was the sickening odor of fish glue at the boiling point. To add to the discomfort, the whole building vibrated from a machine shop on the lower two floors. I could hardly wait for the 6 P.M. siren. The sticker boys—there were about a dozen of us—worked under the stern and often bloodshot eye of a foreman named Meyer, a former sergeant in the German Army. . . . He called [us] "Verfluchter Hund," "Schweinhund," and "Lausbub" (cursed dog, pig-dog and louse-brat). I was almost always a "Lausbub."

The flags, each about the size of a postcard, were printed twelve dozen to a sheet, and Herr Meyer's job was to cut them apart, using a heavy, brass-edged ruler, and then to arrange them in gross lots for the sticker boys. It was tedious work. . . . Almost invariably, when he was angry, he would shuffle across the floor and hit one of us sticker boys on the head with his brass ruler.

Street trades drew a great number of immigrant children. William Zorach was eight when he started as a wage earner, selling papers and shining shoes on the streets of Cleveland. He used to get up at 6 A.M. to go on his paper route. That career ended one stormy winter morning when his mother said, "You can't go out on a day like this." Later, at twelve, he wandered the town looking for "Boy Wanted" signs. The jobs he got, nobody else wanted.

They never lasted more than a few days or a week. . . . I got a machine shop job; a boy told me, "Watch yourself. The last kid working that punch machine lost all his fingers on one hand." I stuck a bar into the machine and broke it. I was fired. I had a job in a hat factory and got bored to death dusting hats. There was a job in a brass factory working with buffing wheels in an atmosphere dense with metal dust, which filled the lungs and eyes and left one coated from head to foot with brass. My job was to dip the hot brass in benzine and roll it in sawdust. It was so painful to the hands that I was in agony. I quit.

The pain young Zorach felt was hidden from public sight. Yet this was the social reality: children degraded and destroyed by conditions of production which no human being should have to bear. Florence Kelley, the daughter of a Pennsylvania congressman who served the interests of his state's iron and steel masters, grew up to defend industry's victims. After an education at Cornell and in Europe, she moved into Chicago's Hull-House settlement. The sur-

Millions of boys and girls supplied cheap labor in the immigrant
decades. To expose their exploitation, Lewis W. Hine took his
camera into the streets and mills. This youngster is carrying a
bundle of "homework" to his tenement family

rounding conditions of slum life horrified her. When Governor Altgeld appointed her chief factory inspector for Illinois in 1893, she exposed the effects of factory labor upon the health of children.

It is a lamentable fact . . . that children are found in greater number where the conditions of labor are most dangerous to life and health. Among the occupations in which children are employed in Chicago, and which most endanger the health, are: the tobacco trade, nicotine poisoning finding as many victims among factory children as among the boys who are voluntary devotees of the weed, consumers of the daily cigarette included; frame gilding, in which work a child's fingers are stiffened and throat disease is contracted; button-holing, machine-stitching and hand-work in tailor or sweat shops, the machine work producing spinal curvature, and for girls pelvic disorders also, while the unsanitary condition of the shops makes even hand-sewing dangerous; bakeries, where children slowly roast before the ovens; binderies, paper-box and paint factories, where arsenical paper, rotting paste, and the poison of the paints are injurious; boiler-plate works, cutlery works, and metal-stamping works, where the dust produces lung disease; the handling of hot metal, accidents; the hammering of plate, deafness. In addition to the diseases incidental to trades, there are the conditions of bad sanitation and long hours, almost universal in the factories where children are employed.

The Kelley report went on to detail many examples of the reckless injury done to children in the shops. Joseph Poderovsky, fourteen, was one of them. Running a heavy buttonhole machine by foot power, he came down with double lateral curvature of the spine. Or there was Bennie Kelman, a young Russian Jewish immigrant who had been put to work in a boiler factory at thirteen. Lifting heavy masses of iron had given him a severe rupture, but nothing had been done for him. He could read only Yiddish. His parents knew no English either, nor where to turn for help until Kelley's inspectors came across Bennie and hospitalized him.

Many children worked in the sweatshops, often alongside their parents. To quit school and go to work, a boy or girl had to be sixteen and obtain working papers. The law was no barrier, said Sam Liptzin.

All the immigrants had plenty of old-country experience in faking the age of their children, either up or down. So it was that many 12- and 14-year-old children, of both sexes, were "accelerated" into the sweatshops. There was a saying among the immigrants, "If I only had ten or twelve children I could open up my own little shop . . ."

Mr. Bobrich was one of these lucky ones with a houseful of nine children. There was only seven years difference between the oldest and the youngest. (Two sets of twins.) All the children worked in the shop with their father, even the one with the crippled hand, who earned a few pennies a day by running errands for the men in the shop.

Mr. Bobrich kept the door to his establishment locked at all times, in order to keep out truant officers. He was constantly paying graft to one official or another on this account. But the best preventive was, of course, not to get caught red-handed violating the law, hence the locked door. At least it gave him a fighting chance to "hide the evidence."

Jane Addams, the Chicago social worker, was bitter about parents "who hold their children in a stern bondage which requires a surrender of all their wages and concedes no time or money for pleasures." But what choice did poor families have? At the wages they worked for, they could not afford to send their children to school. Women and children too had to work to keep the household going. The whole family was sacrificed to the greed of the manufacturers.

Jacob Riis, a Danish immigrant who arrived penniless in New York in 1870 and made himself into a crusading reporter, found poverty and child labor yoked together on the Lower East Side, as everywhere. Whether Jewish, Italian, or Slavic, the sweatshop workers were exploited in the same way. Riis tells of what he discovered when he dropped in on a sweatshop employing Jews.

From among 140 hands in two big lofts in a Suffolk Street factory we picked 17 boys and 10 girls who were patently under 14 years of age, but who all had certificates, sworn to by their parents, to the effect they were 16. One of them whom we judged to be between 9 and 10, and whose teeth confirmed our diagnosis—the second bicuspids in the lower jaw were just coming out— said that he had worked there "by the year." The boss, deeming his case hopeless, explained that he only "made sleeves and went for the beer." Two of the smallest girls represented themselves as sisters, respectively 16 and 17, but when we came to inquire which was the oldest, it turned out that she was the 16-year one. Several boys scooted as we came up the stairs. When stopped, they claimed to be visitors. . . .

In an Attorney Street pants factory we counted 13 boys and girls who could not have been of age, and on a top floor in Ludlow Street, among others, two brothers, sewing coats, who said that they were 13 and 14, but, when told to stand up, looked so ridiculously small as to make even their employer laugh. Neither could read, but the oldest could sign his name. . . . He was one of the many Jewish children we came across who could neither read nor write. Most of them answered that they had never gone to school. . . . They were mostly the children of the poorest and most ignorant immigrants, whose work is imperatively needed to make both ends meet at home.

There were numerous restrictions on the hiring of minors; the issue of child labor was not ignored in the late nineteenth century. But policing of the law was not effective. Employers avoided giving out accurate data on the age of their workers. In the sweatshops as well as the mines, children were often classified not as workers but as "helpers" to their parents. Contrary to popular belief was the fact that most children who worked were not in the factories. They were in the street trades, occupations not regulated by law. Newsboys, bootblacks, peddlers were considered "independent contractors," not employees.

Critics of child labor who investigated conditions were convinced that putting your children to work meant sentencing them to a lifetime of drudgery. Instead of acquiring knowledge and skills at school, they wore themselves out at dull and repetitive tasks. In 1901 about half of New York State's 1,500,000 children aged five to eighteen did not go to school. Ten percent of these children were factory workers. The others were in street trades. "It is a popular fallacy that bootblacks and newsboys grow up to be major generals and millionaires," said one newspaper. "The majority of them, on the contrary, become porters and barkeepers."

Millionaires?

A study of 160 families on the Lower East Side, made by the doctor who treated them all, showed the average *total* wage—the earnings of parents and children combined—was $5.99 per week. The highest family wage was $19, earned by three persons. The lowest was $1.50, earned by a woman in the needle trades.

The cheap labor offered by women and children depressed the general wage scale. The tendency was for the real income of a *family* to approach what an *individual* had earned previously. The old saw "Heaven will protect the working girl" must have meant that no one else would. In New York in the 1880s, women's pay averaged only half as much as men's.

Few Jewish women worked in factories before the 1880s. A decade later about 20,000 of them, mostly American-born, were employed in stores, offices, and schools. The immigrant women now arriving usually worked in tenement sweatshops. As legislation restricted the sweatshops, production of women's clothing in factories expanded, and drew young Jewish women in rapidly growing numbers. Their wages in 1890 ran from $2 to $4.50 a week, a level frequently reduced by heavy fines for trivial offenses. But there were girls earning as little as 30 cents a day to pull threads. One sweatshop operator paid women 20 cents to make a dozen flannel shirts. They worked eleven hours in the shop and another four at home, supplying their own thread and paying for their machines out of their wages. Women were paid $1.50 to make a dozen calico wrappers, 25 cents to make a dozen neckties. A dozen was about all you could do in one day.

In his New York World, Joseph Pulitzer tried to help the immigrant women in the shops by telling their story to the public. One of his reporters in 1885 noted what women earned and how they tried to manage on those wages.

The general average [for shirtmakers] is from $5.50 to $6 per week, when work is steady and a girl is at her machine ten hours a day. Cloakmakers average a little higher—from $6 to $7 per week. Fur-sewers about the same. . . . Tailoresses, whose work is hardest and heaviest of all machine sewing, earn from $6 to $7 per week. . . .

Bindery girls average $6 to $7 per week. Paperbox makers do not average more than $6. . . . Milliners earn higher wages than any of the other trades of this class, averaging from $12 to $18 per week. But it must be remembered that theirs is what is known as a "season trade," and their work is good only for three months each in the spring and fall.

By these figures the average pay of working women is shown to be $7 per week. . . . The usual price of a clean hall bedroom in a respectable house, with reasonably good and sufficient food, is $5 per week. . . . Washing at the lowest estimate is 50 cents per week; fire, a necessity in winter, 50 cents more. If lunch is not furnished that will be 60 cents per week, at the very least.

*And if a girl is obliged to ride to and from her work, there
is 60 cents more for carfare.*

How could you manage a budget on such wages?

As the new century began, garment workers were putting
in a fifty-six- to sixty-hour week. Annual earnings ranged
from $500 a year for the less skilled to $900 for the cutters,
the aristocrats of the trade. A study of living standards
made by the Russell Sage Foundation concluded that $800
a year was the minimum needed for a decent way of life in
New York City. It found, however, that incomes went
above $700 only when a family took in boarders or had the
wife and children work too.

The investigators also looked at the way immigrants of
different ethnic origins spent the same range of income.
Italians were compared with Jews. Jews, they reported,
spent more on fuel and light, on doctoring and on charity.
Italians spent more on food, especially on fruit, vegetables,
cereals, and wine for the table, but less than Jews for meat
and fish.

One Jewish family studied had four children between six
months and six years of age. A week's groceries, bought at a
ground-floor store or from pushcarts, included 6 quarts of
milk, 2 pounds of butter, one dozen eggs, 3½ pounds of
sugar, 6 pounds of potatoes, bread and rolls, beef and fish,
¼ pound of coffee, 2 ounces of tea, tiny amounts of cheese,
dried fruit, and Sabbath wine. They spent one dollar a
month for lamplighting gas in summer and two dollars in
winter.

Economists hold that during this immigration period
real wages rose about one third, meaning the standard of
living went up. But immigrants got less than their share of

the benefits. They worked for the lowest pay, and at jobs afflicted by short or irregular working seasons. Garment work especially was highly seasonal. And unemployment caused by depression (1893–97) struck hardest at these workers who were the last to arrive, came with the least skill, and teetered on the edge of subsistence.

One Jewish researcher named A. Schalit decided around 1910 to find out how Eastern European Jews were getting along in America. He gathered economic data in New York, Philadelphia, Boston, and Chicago. His figures showed the average wage of Jewish working women was $6.50 a week. Allowing for dull seasons, he estimated their annual average earnings at $240. Jewish men were earning $12 a week. Their annual income he put at $450.

He then asked what this meant in the light of the Russell Sage figure of $800 a year required for minimum reasonable comfort. He concluded that beyond doubt the average income of the Jewish immigrant family was barely half that. "But," he added, "ideas of Americans and East European Jews on minimum necessities are *not* the same. The poor," he said, "are not on charity, except for hospitalization; they save money, and they send great sums to relatives in Europe each year."

A charge frequently heard was that the Jewish workers had lowered the standard of living. Burton Hendrick, a reporter who investigated the accusation, called it "ridiculous." The Jews, he said, were not pulling the rest of the population down to their level. The truth was "they constantly seek to raise their own." When describing the immigrants, the press always focused on the Lower East Side. But that district, by the early 1900s, was the home of the newly arrived. The ambition of most Jews living there was

The Lewis W. Hine Collection, International Museum of Photography, George Eastman House

Children making garters in a tenement sweatshop. Thousands of such photos taken by Hine were used by the National Child Labor Committee in the long fight to eliminate child labor

to leave it. "In this the children are especially persistent. They quickly outgrow the three- and four-room flat. Their parents may have worked in the sweatshop but they eschew it. The increase of Italian workmen in the clothing trades, and the gradual decrease of the Jews . . . is one of the most striking evidences of economic improvement. Under the pressure of the second generation the old folks pack their goods and leave Hester, Suffolk and Essex Streets for more sanitary and pretentious quarters. The prosperous . . . find their way to Lexington, Madison, Park and Fifth Avenues and the adjoining streets. The great Jewish bourgeoisie, however, lives in Harlem." By 1907 it was made up almost entirely of former Lower East Siders. At least 70,000 had migrated northward in the preceding five years. Even more had crossed into Brooklyn's Brownsville district.

Many Jewish workers, of course, did not climb into the middle class. They were not alone in failing to earn enough to provide a family with the vaunted American standard of living. The Catholic economist John A. Ryan estimated in 1906 that at least 60 percent of adult male wage earners received less than $600 a year. Father Ryan went beyond bread and butter in his progressive thinking. He contended that families deserved more than just enough food, clothing, and shelter to survive. They should be able to obtain sufficient physical necessities to enjoy good health and maintain self-respect. They should have enough put by for savings and insurance. And they should be able to spend for "mental and spiritual culture"—education, books, sports and recreation, membership in church, labor union, club. Finally, he urged, all the good things of life should be paid for from the father's earnings. Wife and children should not have to work to make ends meet.

11 | Run, Do, Work!

Few Eastern European Jews found a living on American farms. In the old country nearly all of them had been town dwellers because the Czar's law prevented them from owning farmland. Some were able to rent orchards and sell their crops to dealers. The law did not keep them from owning cattle, and dairymen were common in the *shtetl*. But the only way for other Jews to farm was to lease land from absentee owners. The desire to have their own piece of land when it had been so long denied them was therefore strong among some of the immigrants.

Jewish projects for colonizing on American soil had been launched well before the Civil War. A few actually materialized, such as Shalom begun in the 1930s by Moses Cohen in Ulster County, New York. They lasted briefly. B'nai B'rith organized a Hebrew Agricultural Society in the 1850s to encourage Jews to take up farming as a vocation. But not until the mass exodus of Eastern European Jews began was agriculture suggested as a solution for the Jewish emigrants.

Soon after the first pogroms of 1881 a movement in

Russia called Am Olam (Eternal People) dedicated itself to redemption by tilling of the soil. Understandably, a people exiled for millennia from their homeland tended to idealize the land. One of the aims of Am Olam was to refute anti-Semitic propaganda that the Jewish people were "unfitted by habit, nature and sentiment for honest toil." The young hero of Abraham Cahan's novel *The Rise of David Levinsky* is inspired by Am Olam's vision: "I saw a fantastic picture of agricultural communes in far-away America, a life which does not know of mine and thine, where all are brothers and all are happy. Previously I had thought that this could be reached only in the future. Now it was going to be realized in the present. And I would be a participant." But neither David nor Cahan himself took part in Am Olam's mission. Nor were there many among the million Jews arriving in America in the last two decades of the nineteenth century who were willing to stray beyond the familiar immigrant quarters. After all, in the old country they had been town folk. And what kind of life would it be if you left relatives and friends? Still, young idealists were induced to join communes at Sicily Island in Louisiana, New Odessa in Oregon, and Cremieux and Bethlehem Judea in South Dakota. All of them failed, despite the ardor of their founders. Their lack of training and practical experience, as well as soils not suited for agriculture, ruined their chances. In Louisiana the Mississippi flooded their land and carried away all they had. In South Dakota there was first the "wheat bug" and then a drought that lasted two hundred days.

Other sponsors stepped in, placing some hundreds of families in New Jersey farm colonies at Alliance, Carmel, and Rosenhayn. These settlements persisted, although with great difficulty. Their nearness to large cities simplified the problem of marketing their products. More important, the colonists began to supplement their income by combining agriculture with the manufacture of clothing. The best example was launched at Woodbine, New Jersey, in 1891 by the Baron de Hirsch Fund. It grew into an industrial Jewish township circled by satellite farms.

In the early 1900s, the Jewish Colonization Association tried to relieve the crowding of Jews in the ghettos of the large Eastern cities by directing immigrants inland. Working with the Jewish Agricultural Society, it managed to settle over 3,000 Jewish families on farms in New England, New York, New Jersey, and regions farther west. More might have been done to select suitable families with care and give them farm training. But any large-scale success was impossible. The time was wrong. How could the new immigrants be expected to settle on the land when the children of native Americans were deserting the farms for the cities? With the general trend away from agriculture, it was a mistake to believe the Jews—or any other immigrant group—would move in the opposite direction. Agricultural colonization would indeed exert great influence on Jewish life. But in Palestine, not in America.

Jewish philanthropy then sought to find nonfarm jobs for Jews outside the ghettos. An Industrial Removal Office was set up. Once the immigrants' fear of the unknown America beyond New York was dispelled and the small Jewish communities scattered over the country were aroused to a sense of their obligation to welcome the newcomers, resettlement began. By the time the Removal operation was shut down in 1922, it had distributed over 100, 000 Jews to more than a thousand places in every state of the Union. Many times more than that number were drawn to those communities when they heard of the satisfactory life of the pioneering immigrants. The presence today of perhaps a million American Jews in so many small towns and villages throughout the country can in part be traced to that program.

Nevertheless, by far the larger part of the Jewish immigrants lived out their lives in the great urban centers. Ever since 1890, at least two out of every three American Jews have lived in the largest cities—New York, Chicago, Philadephia, Los Angeles, Boston. Today New York City alone contains about one third of America's six million Jews.

Whatever occupation the immigrant Jews turned to, at least it was of their own choice. Here in America the Eastern European Jews found the freedom to make a living, a freedom they never enjoyed in the autocratic regimes of the Czar's Russia, the Emperor's Austria-Hungary, or the King's Rumania. The streets of New York did not prove to be paved with gold, but a Jew was not told he could work only at this or that, or only in this place or that. He could try to make a living wherever he chose. But, points out the historian Lucy Dawidowicz, "the freedom to make money became an obsession" for some. It was an end in itself. It began with a good purpose—to raise the children decently, to keep them out of the sweatshops if possible, to lay aside funds for their education and for old age. But in the process of scrambling for money, "family life was neglected, community was disregarded, tradition abandoned."

By 1890 the path to financial success was already clear. A guidebook put out for immigrant Jews gave this advice:

Hold fast, this is most necessary in America. Forget your past, your customs, and your ideals. Select a goal and pursue it with all your might. No matter what happens to you, hold on. You will experience a bad time but sooner or later you will achieve your goal. If you are neglectful, beware for the wheel of fortune turns quickly. You will lose your grip and be lost. A bit of advice for you: Do not take a moment's rest. Run, do, work and keep your own good in mind.

And no wonder. What America did, said a writer of that period, was to substitute for "the ancient tradition of hospitality a system of heartless exploitation and of neglect. . . . The determining factor in our hospitality has been the necessity for laborers—slaves if you will."

For the rank and file of workers in the mass-production industries there was little chance to advance. Those who came unskilled were almost invariably kept at that level. How many of the untrained could develop skills or accumulate the capital to climb the ladder into management or ownership?

But for the Eastern European Jews who entered commerce or the garment trades, the chance proved somewhat better. The sweatshop system of production which centered in the tenements gave the enterprising operator his opening. In the minute division of labor, subcontracting became the key. It was only a step from journeyman to contractor, and another step from contractor to manufacturer. The man with reckless ambition to get ahead needed very little capital and just a few simple machines to get started. For cheap labor he turned to his own people, whose habits and desires he knew well enough to exploit. Out of their skins he sweated his pennies of profit.

Early in 1907 the muckraking journalist Burton J. Hendrick took a look at what the Eastern European Jews had achieved in the business world of New York. "No people," he wrote in *McClure's*, "have had a more inadequate preparation, educational and economic, for American citizenship. . . . Their only capital stock is an intellect which has not been stunted by centuries of privation, and an industry that falters at no task, however poorly paid. In spite of all these drawbacks, the Russian Jew has advanced in practically every direction. His economic improvement is paralleled by that of no other immigrating race."

Hendrick gave some examples of Jews who had climbed from East Side slums to mansions on Fifth Avenue.

Harry Fischel: a Vilna carpenter who arrived in 1884 with 60 cents in his pocket. His first job paid $3, then $6 a week, part of which he sent home to his starving parents. In eighteen months he had saved $250. On that capital he set up as a builder and in a year had piled up $300,000. Now worth $800,000 and built a home next to Andrew Carnegie.

Harris Mandelbaum: fled the pogroms of the early 1880s, started as a calico peddler, then sold clothes to the poor on the installment plan (50 cents a week), saving enough to buy a tenement house. Now he owned twenty parcels of real estate and was worth a million.

Herman Adelstein: a tinsmith, arrived in 1892, found work in a metal shop, became the owner of an iron foundry. Now worth $400,000.

Nathan Hutkoff: a forty-year-old glazier when he came, put in glass lights on the East Side for a pittance, then opened a little glass store on Canal Street. Now one of the largest plate-glass merchants in New York, with a fortune of $400,000.

Bernard Galewski: a cobbler, began repairing shoes in an

alley off Orchard Street twenty-five years ago at 5 to 25 cents a pair, then went into real estate. Now worth several hundred thousand.

Israel Lebowitz: started as a peddler twenty years ago, then opened a gents' furnishing store on Orchard Street. Now one of the largest shirt manufacturers in the city, with half a million invested in real estate.

Samuel Silverman: once a sweatshop worker, now a cloak manufacturer, with a fortune estimated at $500,000.

S. Friedlander: millinery merchant on Division Street, made $500,000 in twenty-five years.

Etc., etc., etc. . . .

How did it happen?

Hendrick attributed it to two marked characteristics in the Russian Jew.

He is a remorseless pace-maker. He allows himself no rest or recreation, and works all hours of the day and night. He saves every penny, will constantly deny himself and his family nutritious food, and until he has made his mark will live in the most loathsome surroundings. Whether a child in the primary schools, the bent stitcher in the sweatshops, the manufacturer, the merchant, the professional man: constant industry, the determination to succeed—that is his only law. Again, he is an individualist. . . . There is tremendous energy, but it is expressed individually and not collectively. The Jew constantly strives to get ahead; to him the competitive system is the industrial ideal.

Only a comparatively few of the Jews who began with packs on their backs or standing behind pushcarts were still at those "traditionally Jewish" trades, Hendrick said.

The great mass have been living refutations of a popular anti-Semitic libel—that the Jew is congenitally a money-changer, a trader, and not a workman, a manufacturer, an actual producer of wealth. New York's great Jewish community has always supported itself by the labor of its own hands. It is the city's largest productive force and the greatest contributor to its manufacturing wealth. The Russian Jew had not been here many years before he had worked himself up, in large numbers, into all the productive industries. By thousands he took to rolling cigars, making paper boxes, manufacturing surgical instruments, wrought-iron articles, lamps, hardware, cut-glass, practically all the ready-made woodwork used in the building trades, proprietary medicines, drugs, leather goods, cutlery, furniture, upholstery, wagons, harness—indeed, it would be hard to find a manufacturing field in which he has not succeeded. His greatest triumph, of course, has been his absolute control of the clothing industry. It is the largest industry of New York. It employs 175,000 craftsmen, who annually turn out a product valued at $300,000,000. It manufactures more than half of all the wearing apparel—men's and women's suits, cloaks, overcoats, underwear, hosiery, neckties, collars and cuffs, shoes, slippers, etc.—used in the United States. Its predominant factors are now the Russian Jews.

The profits made in manufacture or commerce were often invested in real estate. "The East Side," Hendrick observed, "is possessed of an unending earth hunger. Wherever you see a Russian Jew, however insignificant his station, you see a prospective landlord." Prestige came from acquiring wealth; the form of wealth most esteemed was real estate. On the East Side, tenement properties ranged from $35,000 to $50,000 each in the early 1900s. Yet thousands of immigrant Jews managed to acquire them. How? Hendrick traces the process.

First they became lessees. By constant saving the East Sider gets together $200 or $300 with which, as security, he gets a four or five years' lease of a house. He moves his own family into the least expensive apartment. He himself acts as janitor; his wife and daughters as scrubwomen and housekeepers. He is his own agent, his own painter, carpenter, plumber, and general repair man. Thus he reduces expenses to the minimum. He lets out apartments by the week, always calling promptly himself for the rent. By thus giving constant attention to his work, he has, perhaps, a few hundred dollars every year as a profit. By the time his lease expires, this has swollen to a few thousand. With this he buys a tenement outright. He puts down from $3,000 to $5,000 on a $45,000 building, giving one, two, three, sometimes four mortgages in payment of the rest. Then he repeats his old operation: moves into the cheapest flat, presses his family into service, cuts down all possible expenses, and gives the property his own immediate supervision. When the third or fourth mortgage comes due, he has invariably made enough out of the building to pay it off. He keeps on hard at work and likewise pays off the third and second. Then, as his rents still come in, he invests them in more tenements; until, as a monument to a life spent in the hardest sacrificial toil, he may own a string scattered all over the town.

Jews who could not scrape together the few hundred dollars for a start often combined their smaller savings in a syndicate to acquire a property. Eventually, as it earned profits, each associate might become a prosperous land-holder. Jews who had ventured into other fields often speculated on the side in real estate. With as little as twenty-five dollars, men and women took a hand in the game. As new subways, tunnels, and bridges linked the central city with the outlying districts, thousands of hitherto unreachable acres became habitable. Jews bought up old estates, parceled them out, and reaped the profits. Jewish builders put up block after block of apartments. Immigrants moving on up left the Lower East Side for Harlem, Washington Heights, Brownsville, Williamsburg, and the Bronx. The construction business, once controlled by old native stock, and then by the Irish and the Germans, was coming almost entirely into the hands of the Jews. They built not only housing but hotels, factories, and office buildings. The contractors drew their fellow immigrants in as workmen. The Harry Fischel who could afford to build a home on Fifth Avenue and make himself neighbor to An-drew Carnegie encouraged Jews to enter the building trades by giving them the Sabbath holiday at half pay.

In scarcely twenty-five years Eastern European Jews ac-quired holdings valued in the hundreds of millions. In the Jewish quarter of the Lower East Side, "the former starving subjects of the Czar now hold 70 percent of all the land," Hendrick reported in 1907. It was land once owned largely by the great estates—Astor, Stuyvesant, Whitney. The sixty blocks of Harlem real estate bounded by 110th and 125th streets and Seventh and Lenox avenues were con-trolled mostly by Jews. It happened this way, said Hendrick, because the Jews "have shown themselves the fittest to survive." Others interpreted this to mean the Jews were bloodsucking landlords, squeezing higher rents out of their tenants than other landlords and giving them worse quarters to live in. But in Hendrick's opinion the Jews were not responsible for the city's slum problem. The tenements were terrible, yes, but they had been there decades before the Jewish immigration began. Housing conditions were as bad or worse in the 1850s and 1860s, when non-Jews owned everything. No landlords were more neglectful of their tenants than Trinity Church, the heart of a huge real-estate empire.

Nor, for that matter, were any of the immigrant businessmen in the same financial league as the vestrymen of Trinity Church. Most of the Eastern European Jews who became capitalists were only "crumb-gatherers on the periphery of the American economy," as Judd Teller put it. Some played not insignificant roles in their corner of the stage, but taken as a whole, they were secondary figures. In no way could they be compared with the robber barons who dominated the headlines: Morgan, Rockefeller, Fisk, Gould, Harriman, Astor, Mellon, Hill, Carnegie—non-Jews all, whose wealth and power were enormous. The precarious position of many of the Jewish newly rich crumbled when the Great Depression of the 1930s set in.

In these concluding lines from a Morris Rosenfeld song, an immigrant ground down by the sweatshops warns new arrivals of what America holds in store for them.

Gelt fil un koyech, a gazlen, a
  rotseyech,
Dos fodert amerike haynt.

Yoysher un varhayt, libe un
  klarhayt,
Leyder, dos hot men shoyn
  faynt.
A man fun gevisn, fun ere un
  recht,

A mentsh mit a mentshleche
  herts—
Brider, dem iz in amerike
  schlecht,
Zayn shikzal iz tsores un shmerts.
. . . Doch gibn mir tsu, as
  frayhayt un ru,
Hobn mir do mer vi iberal.

Fun libe un fridn, far kristn un
  idn,
Tsaygt zich undz do yetst a
  shtral.

A lot of money and power, a
  gangster, a robber,
That's what America demands
  today.
Justice and truth, love and
  knowledge,
Alas, that is now hated.

A man with a conscience, honor,
  and justice,

A man with a human heart—

Brothers, for him it is bad in
  America,
His fate is trouble and pain.
Yet we must admit, that
  freedom and security,
We have more of here than
  anywhere else.

Of love and peace for Christians
  and Jews,
There now shines a ray here.

12 | From Greenhorn to American

What went into the making of an American?

Young William Zorach's mother and father came to this country from Russia in their forties. Although they could speak five languages, they had no schooling and could neither read nor write. Stubbornly persisting in being what he was, a Russian Jew, Mr. Zorach never mastered the English language, kept his beard, wore felt boots, and in winter wrapped himself in a huge black overcoat he tied round his waist with a rope.

A few years after settling in Cleveland, the Zorachs sent for their cousins in Russia. "When they arrived," William recalled, "they were dressed in the clothes that children wore in Russia—long pants, boots and gay overshirts with belts. My aunt was scandalized and ashamed of such green-horns. She immediately stripped them of their clothing and dressed them in all new clothes from the store—Americanized them right away."

Mary Antin's father, like William Zorach's aunt, couldn't bear to be thought a greenhorn. He had come to the United States ahead of his family. Now he wrote back to his wife urging her to leave in Polotzk the wig which religion required married Jewish women to wear. Reluctantly she took the first step toward Americanization, starting off for the New World in her own hair.

As soon as she and the children joined Mr. Antin in Boston, they were led to a department store uptown. There, Mary said, they shed their "hateful" homemade European clothes for "real American machine-made garments." They could no longer be pointed out on the streets as greenhorns.

Names were changed as readily as clothes. From Yacov (Hebrew) or Yankel (Yiddish) to Jacob and finally to Jack. From Hyman to Howard, Leybel to Lester or Leon, Berel to Barnett or Barry, Chai-Sura to Sarah, Breina to Beatrice, Simcha to Seymour, Chatzkel to Haskell, Meyer to Max, Moishe to Morris, Aaron to Allan.

Mary Antin tells how it was done in her family.

With our despised immigrant clothing we shed our impossible Hebrew names. A committee of our friends, several years ahead of us in American experience, put their heads together and concocted American names for us all. Those of our real names that had no pleasing American equivalents they ruthlessly discarded, content if they retained the initials. My mother, possessing a name that was not easily translatable, was punished with the undignified nickname of Annie. Fetchke, Joseph, and Deborah issued as Frieda, Joseph, and Dora, respectively. As for poor me, I was simply cheated. The name they gave me was hardly new. My Hebrew name being Mary-ashe in full, Mashke for short, Russianized into Marya, my friends said that it would hold good in English as

Mary; which was very disappointing, as I longed to possess a strange sounding American name like the others.

Everything that typified the old country, in family names as well as first names, had to go. The Russian -skis and -vitches were dropped. Levinsky became Levin, Michaelowitch, Michaels. Russian and Polish names were Anglicized: Bochlowitz to Buckley, Stepinsky to Stevens, Shidlowsky to Sheldon, Horowitz to Herrick, Willinsky to Wilson. Davidowitz became Davidson, Jacobson became Jackson. The Germanic names too were readily translated into English: Weiss-White, Preiss-Price, Reiss-Rice, Rothenberg-Redmont.

Sometimes the decision to change names was not the immigrant's own. Immigration officials at the ports of entry refused to be bothered with exact transcriptions of a new arrival's difficult name. Down on the forms went totally new and easy names—Smith, Jones, Johnson, Robinson, Taylor, Brown, Black, White, Green. And then there were Jews who named themselves after the old streets on the Lower East Side—Clinton, Rivington, Delancey, Rutgers, Stanton, Ludlow. Or when children went to school, teachers who found a name unpronounceable put down on the records something close enough but easier to say. After a time the parents would accept the new name the children brought home.

It was not only a national desire "to be American" like everybody else which accounts for changes in name. Many firms refused to hire people whose names ended in "ski" or "sky." That was "too foreign" for their patrons, was the excuse. If the elite would not trade with or hire people with certain names, then the names were changed. The old folks especially minded the loss of the family name under such conditions. But if it was necessary to make a living . . . And as one East Side patriarch said to a New York *Tribune* reporter in 1898: "We honor our fathers just as much, even if we drop their names. Nothing good ever came to us while we bore them; possibly we'll have more luck with the new names."

In America, the way to success seemed to be the way out of the ghetto. The newcomers were in the minority. They were attracted by the ways of the old and settled majority. "As in a teacup one sees the little bubbles drawn to the larger ones and merging instantly when once in contact, so the larger life tends to absorb the smaller group," wrote one observer, Emily Greene Balch. "Indeed, the prestige of America, and the almost hypnotic influence of this prestige on the poorer class of immigrants, is often both pathetic and absurd. They cannot throw away fast enough good things and ways that they have brought with them, to replace them by sometimes inferior American substitutes."

In thinking back upon his childhood the novelist Saul Bellow regretted the way in which the newcomers imitated what they found here.

> It was common in that generation and the next to tailor one's appearance and style to what were, after all, journalistic, publicity creations, and products of caricature. The queer hunger of immigrants and their immediate descendants for true Americanism has yet to be described. It may be made to sound like fun, but I find it hard to think of anyone who underwent the process with joy. Those incompetents who lacked mimetic talent and were pure buffoons were better off—I remember a

cousin, Arkady, from the old country who declared that his new name was now, and henceforth, Lake Erie. A most poetic name, he thought.

Eventually, Cousin Arkady simply became Archie and "made no further effort to prove himself a real American." Others did not give up so easily. A greater obstacle to overcome than name or clothing was language. The tongue he spoke singled out the "greener." Yiddish was the badge of an alien culture; English was the proper language for an American. The place to learn it was in school, obviously, but not everyone could go. Walking the streets of Philadelphia in search of a job, Nathan Kuskin tried to learn English by reading the signs and billboards.

I was puzzled by the many words spelled differently from their pronunciations. In Russian every consonant and vowel is pronounced as written, but in this strange language I found wide variations. . . . The reading of signs on stores gave me wrong impressions about many things. For instance, I had an idea that "Mr. Ice Cream" was a multi-millionaire chainstore owner because I had seen so many stores with his name on them. To accelerate my learning, on Sunday mornings . . . I would walk over to any church on Broad Street, not to pray, but to listen to the sermon and thus add a few words to my vocabulary. If I did not understand a word I would memorize it and later look it up in my pocket Russian-English dictionary.

Kuskin entered a night school for workers, paying five dollars for a year's course in English. Working hard all day in a cigar shop and studying every night proved too much.

He joined with several other immigrants to hire a private tutor. They met once a week to read a book together and discuss it in English.

The impatient Abraham Cahan started even earlier, on the way to America. He picked up a German-English dictionary before boarding ship and on the thirteen-day voyage used it to help the immigrants explain their needs to the ship's officers. For a while he struggled alone with English grammar, then decided he needed a more solid grounding. He went to an East Side elementary school and for several months sat with a class of twelve-year-olds. A year later this immigrant knew enough English to be able to tutor other immigrants.

This zest for education had ancient roots. The Jews were probably the first people to aspire to total literacy—at least for the males. It rose out of the religious obligation to study the Bible and Talmud as the pathway to God. The greatest prestige went to religious scholars. If a man stayed illiterate and ignorant his religious piety was questioned. So universal education for males was a critical goal of Jewish society. The hope was to educate each man to the limit of his ability. And when formal education ended, it was his obligation to continue study on his own. The more learning, the more life. Study made you into a human being.

Of course, the learning to be sought was Jewish learning, religious learning. To acquire knowledge of the secular world was a personal choice. But once the Enlightenment took hold, secular learning began to undermine Jewish learning. The secular scholars said you couldn't understand the world unless you went beyond the mastery of Jewish culture. And well before the mass migration of Eastern European Jews began in the 1880s, secular education had begun to change the lives of many. The fervent dedication to religious study was transposed to worldly study. So explosive was the effect upon intellectuals of Jewish origin that Jews were making enormous contributions to science and scholarship well before World War I.

The millions of Eastern European Jews who migrated to the United States seized upon the freedom to go to school as a right to be cherished as passionately as the freedom to make a living. And the two became linked, for secular education was seen as the door to success in the New World. In Russia, Jews were denied equal opportunity in the schools. Here the public schools were open to all. You did not have to bribe an official or convert to Christianity to get into school.

The economic rewards of education were not a paramount consideration in the old country. Here, for many, success became synonymous with prosperity. The American commitment to education, initiated by the Protestant culture, was strengthened by the great influx of Jews. Family status was held to be dependent upon it. Not only by the first generation to come, but by their American-born children, who in this respect did not rebel against a powerful family value. Other immigrant groups might permit or encourage their children to evade compulsory schooling. But not the Jews. As a group they made an almost superhuman effort to acquire the education and culture America offered.

Mary Antin was one of about a hundred "green" children who started school in Boston's Chelsea neighborhood in 1894. Her proud father himself brought his four children the first day, "as if it were an act of consecration." He had written his family repeatedly that his chief hope for his children was free education, "the essence of American opportunities, the treasure that no thief could touch, not even misfortune or poverty." As for Mary's feelings, she was, she said, "carried along by a tremendous desire to learn, and had my family to cheer me on." She was put in the second grade, under Miss Nixon.

There were about half a dozen of us beginners in English, in age from six to fifteen. Miss Nixon made a special class of us, and aided us so skillfully and earnestly in our endeavors to "see-a-cat," and "hear-a-dog-bark," and "look-at-the-hen," that we turned over page after page of the ravishing history, eager to find out how the common world looked, smelled, and tasted in the strange speech. The teacher knew just when to let us help each other out with a word in our own tongue—it happened that we were all Jews—and so, working all together, we actually covered more ground in a lesson than the native classes, composed entirely of the little tots.

Like Mary Antin, Samuel Chotzinoff started school in the second grade, but on the Lower East Side. His mother fitted him out with an oblong pencil box (ten cents), four writing pads (a penny each), and a set of colored blotters (a nickel). The graying, middle-aged Miss Murphy had fifty boys to teach.

She was severely distant, and her impersonal attitude, added to the formality of being called by our last names, cast a chill on the classroom. Soon one began to long for the sound of one's first name as for an endearment that would, at a stroke, establish a human relationship between oneself and Miss Murphy. But it was not to be.

> . . . *Notwithstanding Miss Murphy's frigidity, she soon commanded our interest and respect, and we made good progress in reading and spelling. . . .*
>
> *Miss Murphy, who read aloud to us, appeared neither interested in nor moved by the McGuffey stories. She read without nuances and exhibited no emotion. Completely indifferent to the music of poetry, she would recite a line like the exquisite, "How would I like to go up in a swing, up in the air so blue!" in a cold, earthbound voice, look up from her book, and say, "Plotkin, spell swing." Yet she was an excellent disciplinarian, and our class speedily gained a reputation for good spelling.*

Public School No. 1 at the corner of Catherine and Henry streets was a big white building trying to educate what one reporter described as "the miserably poor polyglot population" of the East Side district. Among the twenty-five-odd ethnic groups sending their children to it were the Swedes, Austrians, Greeks, Armenians, Irish, Welsh, Italians, Poles, Germans, Chinese, Russians. The Jewish children predominated.

To teach such classes must have been a great challenge. What Harry Roskolenko remembers of P.S. 31 is the discipline invoked.

> *Schooling in my time, at P.S. 31, was very stern. The teacher, though not a cop, was nevertheless a ruler-wielding teacher. We knew the ruler because it was often applied to our asses by both teacher and principal. We would get slapped, and they were right. I was never right at any time—said my parents, who were immediately told of each incident by a note from the teachers or the principal. They sided with the teachers, and my report card proved that I was sleeping when I should have been*

studying. I was left back—*a phrase that became quite
familiar around our house. . . . Nevertheless, all of us
learned quickly. There was no easy route to high school
and college.*

P.S. 79 was the grammar school J. R. Schwartz attended
on the Lower East Side. Long after the red brick building
on First Street had been turned into a warehouse, he could
still recall almost every teacher he had, beginning at the top.

*I still remember Mr. Phripp, the principal, a tall rangy
individual, with a pointed, sandy-colored Van Dyke
beard and a bulbous, gigantic nose. Every morning with
all classes at assembly he read a portion of the Bible in
his benign voice. At first blush he gave the impression of
utter goodness, a goodness that was a mask for a vindic-
tive nature. Woe unto him who was unfortunate enough
to be sent by his teacher to his office with a note for
some infraction of school discipline. . . . Mr. Phripp
was harsh, unrelenting and satanically lavish in doling
out punishment.*

*My first teacher at P.S. 79 was Miss Reilly. In the
succeeding term I had a Miss Keilly. Then as the grades
advanced and we changed to the departmental form, I
had Miss Donovan, she with the strabismic eyes, as my
regular class teacher. She was nicknamed "Cockeye"
Donovan. Miss Keilly was blessed with a satanic smirk.
Mr. Collins, who taught American literature, must have
been afflicted with adenoids. He talked with a nasal
twang. Mr. Patsy Beamer taught algebra and Mr.
Krampner arithmetic and English. Mr. Ruskin had
charge of the elementary physics class and Mrs. Deve-
reaux, the first-year French. Then there was a Mr. Fish, a
little man with a large, sandy-haired head and red face*

who substituted for any teacher who would be absent from class. And finally, Mr. Foster, who taught shop work. Mr. Foster was never known to crack a smile. He was a little pompous man who took himself very seriously. . . . Mr. Telluson, who also taught English, was a kindly man who seemed to understand us and went out of his way to make us see the beauty in poetry.

Mr. Krampner was the only Jewish teacher on the staff until Mr. Ruskin showed up, from Russia via London, where he must have adopted the respected name of the British art of critic.

He endeared himself to the pupils because on Saturdays he would invite different groups to his home where we all sat around on the floor and he expounded to us the wonders of nature and science. When the weather was clement he would take us to the various parks of the city "to hold communion with nature in her visible forms."

Teachers, the immigrant children learned, were not all of a piece. When Morris R. Cohen started school in Brooklyn his first teacher was a Mrs. Phinney. She opened the day by asking all the boys to recite with her the Lord's Prayer. He didn't like it, but he didn't dare protest. And when she scolded a classmate and said to him, "Don't walk like a sheeny," young Morris was depressed. It was bad enough that the boys called the few Jews in the class by that name. But before long he and Mrs. Phinney became very good friends: she proved to be an imaginative and caring teacher who brought out the best in her pupils. He could overlook her prejudices.

His last year of high school (it was 1894–95) was one of

"great intellectual as well as physical awakening" for fifteen-year-old Morris Cohen. He met the masterpieces of English and American literature, discovering that not only novels but essays and history and poetry were revelations of marvelous new worlds. By the year's end he was thrilled to be reading Plato. Benjamin Franklin's *Autobiography* gave him the happy and practical notion of keeping a record of his intellectual progress by jotting down the day's thoughts in a diary. When he won a gold medal for the highest mark scored on a college entrance examination, his mother cried. Not because of the medal, but because it meant her son could go to college. When one of his aunts remonstrated, "You can't afford to send your son to college," she replied, "If need be I'll go out as a washerwoman and scrub floors so that my Morris can have a college education."

For Maurice Hindus the first "truly American world" that opened to him was Stuyvesant High School. It educated boys from all the boroughs, rich and poor. There was at that time only a sprinkling of immigrants like himself. The boys were clean and well dressed, and excited by sports in a way he couldn't understand. Unlike most of them, Maurice worked long hours in a shop after classes and on Saturdays. He tells why the school was an adventure for him.

> *It was not the students as much as the teachers who stirred my imagination. There was nothing of the stiffness and severity of Russian teachers about them. The manual training teachers did not mind soiling their hands with greasy tools or with paint. They showed no feudal disdain of menial work. They never made students aware of a social gulf between them, which made*

> *the school a lively and happy community, though not untouched by the petty rivalries, the exuberant roughness, the guileful rogueries that now and then seize teenage boys. . . .*
>
> *I soon discovered that in my relationship with teachers my immigrant origin instead of being a liability was a real asset. English was my favorite subject and I couldn't have had more helpful and generous-spirited instructors. . . . If I wrote a composition that pleased them, they were lavish with praise in their written comments and often spoke to me after class, advising me what books to read and encouraging me to write.*

Hindus won first prize in the annual short-story contest for sophomores. From reading so much English literature he became, he said, "passionately Anglophile."

The training of future citizens, everyone agreed, was the first duty of the public schools. And to speak and write English well was the primary path to that goal. The children of the Jewish immigrants heard Yiddish at home, a mixture of many languages on the street, plus the latest American slang, and "proper" English for only five hours of the day in school. But the result of training after only five or six years in school was "wonderful," reported the New York *Evening Post* in 1903. Not only for the pupils, it went on, but for their parents, who learned daily the rudiments of English through the medium of their children. The method used at school was constant drill in enunciation and pronunciation. The best pupils were chosen to speak at assemblies; they set models of good English for the others, while competing for medals for excellence.

Just as important as learning English, said the *Post*, was

learning the absolute necessity of cleanliness for good health in children. A major task of the teacher was to insist upon clean hands and faces, combed hair, and shined shoes or boots. Monitors stood at assembly doors to see that the pupils passed inspection.

The study of civics and American history was foremost for citizenship education. Besides the class work, the training called for the recitation of patriotic pieces at the morning assembly, the singing of patriotic songs, and the daily salute to the flag. Special exercises to honor national holidays were red-letter days in school life. Army generals were brought in to fire up assemblies with their memories of Civil War days.

The largest public school in the world—P.S. 188—was located on the Lower East Side. Five thousand boys and girls jammed its ninety-six classrooms. When a *Tribune* reporter visited the school in 1906, he asked a class of thirty-eight boys (average age fourteen, and the majority Jewish) what they wanted to be when they grew up. Eleven said, go into business; nine intended to be lawyers; six, civil engineers; three, doctors; three, dentists; two, teachers; and one each, electrical engineer, mechanic, clothing designer, and engraver.

Special classes were provided for children just off the boat. One such class the reporter looked in on held thirty-three girls, all Jewish and about thirteen years old. Twenty had been born in Russia, seven in Hungary, and six in Austria. Half had arrived in New York in the last six months, fleeing the recent pogroms. "Do they appreciate the opportunities of this country?" asked the reporter. The teacher put the question to Rosie in Yiddish. Her answer, translated, was: "I love sweet America. They are kind to me here."

13 | The Melting Pot Leaks

"They are kind to me here."

They tried to be, many of them. But did they know how? They—the older Americans, the ones who had come here earlier and who had acquired wealth and position and power—they determined public policy. They shaped the schools. And they were white Protestants. Naturally their success made them believe they were the best. Whatever they had become in their American existence was to be the model for the newcomers pouring into the Golden Land.

So when the public schools dedicated themselves to "Americanizing" the masses of immigrants from Eastern and Southern Europe, they had in mind the manners, the style, the culture, the morals, the values of the solidly entrenched white Protestant elite, chiefly the New England Yankees. One of the leading educators of the time said the major task of the schools was "to break up those [immigrant] groups of settlements, to assimilate and amalgamate these people as part of our American race, and to implant in their children, so far as can be done, the Anglo-Saxon conception of righteousness, law and order, and popular government."

You can make it here, he was saying, if you will only become "real" Americans. Drop what makes you different. Forget where your parents came from, what they brought with them, their own feelings and experience, their own beliefs and values.

As the immigrants continued to pour in, the magazine *Scientific American* urged them to "assimilate" quickly or face "a quiet but sure extermination." If you keep your alien ways, it warned, you "will share the fate of the native Indian."

How wrong this attitude was, only a few understood. Jane Addams, the founder of Hull-House in the Chicago slums, was one of them. She wrote:

> *The public school too often separates the child from his parents and widens the old gulf between fathers and sons which is never so cruel and so wide as it is between the immigrants who come to this country and their children who have gone to the public school and feel that there they have learned it all. The parents are thereafter subjected to certain judgment, the judgment of the young which is always harsh and in this instance founded upon the most superficial standard of Americanism.*

As far back as 1908, Jane Addams urged the schools:

> *. . . to do more to connect these children with the best things of the past, to make them realize something of the beauty and charm of the language, the history and the traditions which their parents represent. . . . It is the business of the school to give to each child the beginnings of a culture so wide and deep and universal*

that he can interpret his own parents and countrymen by a standard which is worldwide and not provincial.

I know what she meant. For as the son of immigrants I can see now what I missed in the schools I went to. My parents had come from Eastern Europe just before the turn of the century. Many of the children I went to school with in Massachusetts were the first American-born generation. My parents, like those of most of my schoolmates, had only the most rudimentary schooling in the old country. They were in a grand rush to become Americans. My mother had come here at fourteen, my father at eighteen. They did not want to be ridiculed as greenhorns, and as Yiddish was the badge of foreignness, they spoke so little of their own tongue that I learned scarcely a word of it. They told me nothing of their own years in Eastern Europe. Was it because they wanted to forget the world they had left behind? Or because they thought I had no interest in their culture?

Whatever the reason, I learned little about my people's past in my home. And nothing at all in my school. The schools stripped the immigrant children of their Old World heritage. We felt embarrassed by the language of our ancestors. Their history, their traditions, were not thought worthy of study. America was the land of the Anglo-Saxon Protestant elite. Our own ethnic identity was swept under the rug. I felt myself an outsider. What happened to me was not unique. What child without an Anglo-Saxon name or skin has not felt himself an outsider? We were given nothing to make us sure of ourselves and proud of what we were.

For the goal of the schools was to Americanize the newcomers. That meant to shape us into loyal and patriotic citizens. But it was an uncritical Americanization. We were not taught to ask questions about this country and its institutions. Julia Richman thought that was wrong. The first woman to be made a district superintendent of schools in New York City, she chose to work on the Lower East Side. How can we demand uncritical Americanization of these children, she said, when all around them is a "general corruption of municipal government" and a "general un-ethical basis of the commercial world?" She too, like Jane Addams, believed that an Americanization which blanked out the history of immigrant children was wrong.

In popular thought America has been glorified as a melt-ing pot of different peoples. But apart from whether or to what degree this happened, was it a good idea? When it meant melting diversity into conformity with Anglo-Saxon characteristics? If you were unable to do it or didn't want to go along, then you were abused or shut out because middle-class America accepted only those who conformed to their super-culture. Everyone else was but a "spick," "mick," "dago," "greaseball," "hunkie," "Polack," "nig-ger," "Yid." Their race, their religion, their people's culture made them unworthy of America in the Nordic eyes of the "old Americans." The effect? Michael Novak puts it this way:

> *Under the whiplash of such attitudes, many descen-dants of immigrants for many years withered into silence about their identity. Many suppressed the instincts of their flesh, the impulses of their sensibilities, and per-haps even the signals from their genes. (Teachers made Italian boys sit on their hands all morning long, to make*

them stop gesticulating.) A great many try desperately to
be all alike, *to look the way Americans do in the maga-*
zines, and movies and streets: to make it, to pass.

Among many of the immigrants total assimilation
seemed contrary to the spirit of democracy. To them democracy meant freedom to make choices, freedom to be
oneself, and they stubbornly resisted attempts to force
them into the melting pot. The wiping out of their own
culture was too high a price to pay.

But even back then the melting-pot theory did not go
unopposed. Some thinkers pointed out that if the ethnic
groups were not robbed of their cultural differences these
special qualities would enhance American life. More, they
challenged the notion that the immigrant groups which
had come before the 1880s had already lost their identity.
Some or even many individuals, yes, but never the group as
a whole. (Today historians and sociologists agree that
Americanization did not rub out the distinctive traits of the
ethnic groups and create a new American.)

The idea of cultural pluralism was put forth to stress the
desirability of maintaining ethnic variety. Its proponents
argued that to demand cultural homogeneity was as oppressive as to deny the right to freedom of speech or freedom of religion. The immigrant of whatever ethnic origin is
no outsider, they said. The culture of any ethnic group is
rightly part of the ever-changing pattern of culture that
makes up America. Horace M. Kallen, a Jew and a philoso-
pher who was one of the earliest spokesmen for cultural
pluralism, said, "Since people have to live together, plu-
rality is a basic condition of existence. The need is to bring
differences together to make a union, not unity."

Jews particularly, but by no means exclusively, have been aware of their individuality as a people. For how many centuries have they shown how unwilling they are to surrender it? The Poles too, and the Bohemians, the Pennsylvania Germans, the Irish, the Slavs, the Italians, to name only some. All intensely nationalist, even when they rose from proletarian status to prosperity. As they freed themselves from the stigma of "greenhorn," they developed group self-respect and pride. They clung to their language and their religion, maintaining out of worker's wages schools and a press in their national tongue.

Putting aside, for the moment, the failure of the schools to teach the immigrant children something of their heritage, how effective was the education they did try to impart? Much is said today of the decline of the public schools, implying that they were excellent in the "good old days." But "the truth is," writes Colin Greer, "that our public schools have always failed the lower classes—both white and black." In his study *The Great School Legend*, he concludes it is simply not true that the schools took the poor immigrants who crowded into the cities and molded them into the homogeneous productive middle class we claim as America's strength and pride. On the contrary:

> *In virtually every school effectiveness study since the one made in Chicago in 1898, more children have failed in urban public schools than have succeeded, both in absolute and in relative numbers. Among the school systems which had large numbers of immigrants and poor pupils, in Boston, Chicago, Detroit, Philadelphia, Pittsburgh, New York and Minneapolis, failure rates were so high that in no one of these systems did the so-called*

"normal" group exceed 60 percent, while in several instances it fell even lower.

Only a small number of young people got as far as high school in the first place. Scarcely 8 percent aged fourteen to seventeen were high-schoolers in 1900. And of these, only about 12 percent finished and graduated. But the immigrants' children did as well—or as badly—as the children of native-born whites, says the educational historian Edwin A. Krug.

The Jews are often given as the example of immigrant success in the schools. They were one of the ethnic groups who did better than some others. But by no means did all Jews do well. Otherwise, asks Colin Greer, "why the remedial classes and dropout panic in several of the schools on New York's Lower East Side with as much as 99 percent 'Hebrew' registration? Where the family was poor enough to take in boarders to cover rental costs, and desperate enough to join the city's welfare rolls, delinquency and criminality were then, as they are now in some urban neighborhoods, the burden of Jewish families too." The Jews too had their prostitutes, pimps, con men, gangsters, and killers.

As with other ethnic groups, school performance seemed to be tied to the socioeconomic position of the pupil's family. The better off the parents were, the better the child did in the classroom. Greer concludes that those who succeeded rarely did so because of the public schools.

The white working class never climbed upward as rapidly or as surely as it has become traditional to believe, Greer says. The school dropout rates for all groups, including blacks, were tied to "the terrifying vulnerability" of the unskilled labor the parents did. When adult employment fell off, the children dropped out in direct proportion.

Only a few hard facts about the schools of that era are enough to show what the children were up against. City schools were under the control of political bosses who looted education funds. As a result, books and supplies were short and buildings overcrowded. Schools built for a thousand pupils often held double that number. In 1893 one Brooklyn classroom packed in 153 students; many classes had 90 or 100 students. Lighting and ventilation were usually poor. Physical punishment with stick or fist was legal and common. The pupils were force-fed information. Not thinking, but memorization was the accepted path to knowledge. And repetition—endless, deadening repetition—was the way to mastery of the three Rs. Every pupil was considered to be exactly like every other one—a receptacle into which unrelated and meaningless information was mechanically dumped like so much garbage. Spontaneity was suppressed, imagination ridiculed. The pupil could have nothing worthwhile to say; the teacher was the fount of all wisdom.

For the poor there was the added handicap of hunger. A 1905 survey of schoolchildren in four major cities showed one out of every three came to school having had no breakfast or a very poor one. Huge numbers could not learn because they were listless and apathetic; many others could not learn because they were exhausted from long hours of work they had to do outside school hours to help support their families.

And what of the quality of the teachers? Before 1900, teaching was not a true profession. Someone who wanted a teaching job needed only the most brief and casual training or simply political pull. The "normal schools," the forerunners of the teachers colleges, gave better preparation, but many didn't even require high-school diplomas of their students. Of course, there were still teachers with natural talent who cared for the boys and girls entrusted to them. But the patronage, graft, and favoritism which riddled the school system, and the low pay and slow promotion which rewarded their efforts, could discourage even the ablest and most devoted.

If people like Morris R. Cohen have given us happier memoirs of their schooling than this picture suggests, it was because they were extraordinary. The great mass made no mark in the world and have left us no record. We have only the statistics of success and failure to go by, the facts the historians of education have unearthed. The one exception, Colin Greer reports, was the Jews. They were more able than other white ethnic groups to use public education as a way up. But by no means all, he adds.

The public school was the most powerful force for Americanization. It was compulsory, and in some big cities such as New York, it was free from kindergarten right through college. There were two other forces, however, which helped mold the immigrants and their children into the forms of New World life. One was the settlement house and the other the library.

On the Lower East Side the librarians found the appetite of the immigrants for knowledge to be insatiable. Self-education was the most persistent work of the newcomers. A report investigating these "foreign book-worms" in 1913 uncovered this story:

> A *stout, deep-eyed, dark-complexioned Russian came to the librarian of the Seward Park Branch several years ago and asked her for books on advanced chemistry. He*

had read all those available through the library, but lacked enough money to buy the more expensive and technical volumes. His request was similar to those she had frequently heard and she as often had been compelled to refuse. She knew the young man, however, and in a few days interested a chemist from one of the large manufacturing concerns of the city.

In the spirit of adventure this man climbed the stairs of a narrow Canal Street tenement and knocked at the door of an attic room. When the Russian admitted him the visitor stood at the threshold dumbfounded. He thought he was calling at the "bunk" of an immigrant. Instead he walked into a shabby but fully equipped chemical laboratory, hidden under the rafters of a five-story building.

Here was a young man who had been banished from Odessa because he was a Jew. He had sought political and religious freedom in the United States and did his first work in a sweatshop. From there he went to a clothing store, and in the evening tutored himself with public books. The few dollars he could save he spent for instruments.

Not many days after this meeting he was supplied with the latest books. He then passed the Regents' examinations and now is professor of chemistry in a Brooklyn institute.

At the branch libraries serving the East Side non-fiction was reported to be most in demand. Readers asked for economics, philosophy, history, politics. The fiction requested included the works of Dickens, Scott, Thackeray, Dumas, Tolstoy. In one library a hundred copies of *David*

Copperfield were not enough to meet the demand. In 1903 the *Evening Post* sent a reporter to the Chatham Square branch to see how the immigrant children were using it. He found that as soon as school closed at 3 P.M. lines of children formed at the library, reaching down two flights of stairs and into the street.

The children are drawing books in English at the rate of 1,000 a day. Opened four years ago, the branch has 15,000 members. It stands third in the number of its circulation and since its opening has ranked first in the proportion of history and science taken out. It is almost wholly used by Jews. A few Italians from Mulberry Street, a handful of Chinese from Mott and Doyers, and a scanty representation from other races come here occasionally.

Probably the most popular book in the whole library is a history for young people entitled The Story of the Chosen People, *the many copies of which are always traveling raggedly to the bindery. Rivaling it, however, is* Uncle Tom's Cabin. *As the story of an oppressed race it strikes a responsive chord in the Jewish child. Sue's* The Wandering Jew *is another prime favorite.*

The librarians are a constant source of astonishment to the children. A peculiarly cordial spirit pervades the building. Every assistant is interested in her work, for those who are not interested do not stay. In return the children love them all, write them fervid letters of adoration, make them presents, and run their errands. And that the objects of so much sincere admiration should be Christians puzzles their small heads. . . .

The letters written to the librarians by the children

display all the luxuriance of an Oriental imagination. "My dear Miss Sheerin, only God knows how much I love you. I send you as many kisses as there are pennies in the world," wrote one fanatical little adorer.

The Jewish child has more than an eagerness for mental food; it is an intellectual mania. He wants to learn everything in the library and everything the librarians know. He is interested not only in knowledge that will be of practical benefit, but in knowledge for its own sake. Girls and boys under twelve will stand before the library shelves so much absorbed in looking up a new book that they do not hear when spoken to. No people reads so large a proportion of solid reading.

In Boston, Mary Antin discovered the public library in the summertime when school was closed.

The library did not open till one in the afternoon, and each reader was allowed to take out only one book at a time. Long before one o'clock I was to be seen on the library steps, waiting for the door of paradise to open. I spent hours in the reading-room, pleased with the atmosphere of books, with the order and quiet of the place, so unlike anything on Arlington Street. The sense of these things permeated my consciousness even when I was absorbed in a book, just as the rustle of pages turned and the tiptoe tread of the librarian reached my ear, without distracting my attention. Anything so wonderful as a library had never been in my life. It was even better than school in some ways. One could read and read, and learn and learn, as fast as one knew how. . . . When I went home from the library I had a book under my arm; and I would finish it before the library opened next day,

*no matter till what hours of the night I burned my little
lamp.*

Mary read nearly everything that came to hand. Louisa
May Alcott's stories first of all, but boys' books of adventure
too. Anything in print, even the stained old newspapers
which enclosed fish brought home from the market. She
enjoyed the Yiddish newspapers her father subscribed to
and the library's many-volumed encyclopedia, especially for
its sketches of famous people and her favorite authors.
Visiting the main library on Copley Square was a special
treat. She felt it was "my palace—mine!" even though she
was born in Russia and lived in a slum. She spent her
longest hours in the vast reading room.

*Here is where I liked to remind myself of Polotzk, the
better to bring out the wonder of my life. That I who
was born in the prison of the Pale should roam at will in
the land of freedom was a marvel that it did me good to
realize. That I who was brought up to my teens almost
without a book should be set down in the midst of all
the books that ever were written was a miracle as great as
any on record. That an outcast should become a privi-
leged citizen, that a beggar should dwell in a palace—this
was a romance more thrilling than poet ever sang. Surely
I was rocked in an enchanted cradle.*

14 | Settlements in the Slums

Uptown Jewry took an early hand in Americanizing the immigrants downtown. As the flood of newcomers rose, the German Jews realized they had better help the Eastern Europeans. If these "raw and uncivilized" Jews were not assimilated rapidly, non-Jews would identify them with *all* Jews. So the German Jews set out to "uplift, refine, and Americanize" the new arrivals. They backed experimental ventures in kindergartens, in vocational training, in the teaching of English. For many years their major effort would be centered in a new settlement house designed to "dissolve the ghetto" around it. Enough funds were raised by 1891 to open the Educational Alliance, housed in a five-story building at East Broadway and Jefferson Street. Through educational, religious, and civic training, moral and physical culture, the trained staff aimed to better the condition of the Jews on the Lower East Side. From 9 A.M. to 10 P.M. the settlement was open to all who wanted to use its auditorium, gymnasium, shower baths, library, and roof garden.

The Educational Alliance was soon reaching 6,000 Jew-

ish immigrants, two thirds of them children, every week-
day. On weekends more than sixty clubs held meetings in
the building. The children were given intensive lessons
which succeeded, within six months of their landing, in
passing them on to the public schools (which would not
accept them until they were able to use English).

In its early years the Alliance banned the use of Yiddish
within its walls. It gave no encouragement to the expression of the immigrants' own culture. The newcomers were
bathed in an artificial atmosphere of Anglo-Saxon culture.
There were classes in English, in civics, in American history, in the literature of America and England. Bryant,
Longfellow, Lowell, and Emerson were the favorite poets.
The students delved into the ancient worlds of Greece and
Rome, but not the history of the Jew. And like the public
schools, the Alliance waved the flag and preached patrio-
tism on the national holidays.

It took over a decade before the Alliance found links
between the traditional life of ghetto and *shtetl* from
which the immigrants fled and the urban life of modern
New York into which they plunged. The use of Yiddish in
classroom teaching became the bridge between the two.
The Alliance prepared a guidebook in Yiddish (*Sholem
Aleichem tsu immigranten*) for the newcomers and translated the Declaration of Independence into Yiddish. To
the immigrants the Declaration, Franklin's *Autobiography*,
and the Constitution became basic scripture. But "we must
not forget," warned one settlement librarian, "that these
are the children for whose parents were written such dis-
tinctly non-Anglo-Saxon books as *Anna Karenina*, *Crime
and Punishment*, and *Taras Bulba*." She did not want to
see her young Russian-Jewish patrons denied their heritage.

The many other settlement houses which sprang up in New York took the same nonsectarian position as the Alliance. Their intent was to bring the multi-ethnic New Yorkers together, not stress what they feared (mistakenly) might keep them apart. By the end of the century there was a string of new settlement houses running up the East Side: the University Settlement, the Henry Street Settlement, the College Settlement, Madison House, Clark House, Christadora House. . . .

As early as the age of seven, the Educational Alliance became for Harry Roskolenko the place where he learned to become a junior carpenter, remaking his Russian-Jewish home with bookcases, stool, chinning bar, and towel rack. In the crowded Alliance classes he studied subjects he couldn't get, at his young age, in public school.

The Jacob A. Riis Collection, Museum of the City of New York

On the roof playground of one of New York's settlement houses, organized by the Hebrew Institute

Carpenter, about-to-be-mariner, Boy Scout, I knew about birds, flowers, tides, rocks—and how to repair a broken head, with bandages. For the Educational Alliance taught a sullen or a happy boy to be less violently errant, more decently dutiful, and almost properly American—with our East Side local combinations. It was an alliance of American hope plus universal scope. All a boy student had to do was go there, try not to beat up the then-tough teachers—and he was due to become a doctor in twenty years, so well trained that he would never be sued for malpractice.

If you were a sickly, pale, underweight, bronchial boy and your mother was a talking baleboosteh, *she quickly convinced one of the Alliance's many extraterritorial departments that her son, about to die from every known form of undernourishment, must have a two-week free vacation at Surprise Lake Camp, some miles from New York, in middling mountains, with natural cows, and a lake to swim in. . . .*

There was a Mother's Department at the Alliance, hoping to teach young mothers to become older mothers, and another department for girls interweaving between the alerted mothers. There were sewing classes, homemaking studies, dance socials, and gymnasiums— but nothing about sex. It was a taboo subject. . . .

There was music at the Alliance, with fiddlers, pianists, and quartets; and there were children's study halls, men's reading rooms, a religious education department, for Torah studies, as well as Yiddish, Hebrew, Russian— and accented Litvak. One day a boy running between his house and the Alliance's many cultural departments would cease to run, and become the man his father was not—a cultured American.

Out of the Alliance's art classes came such distinguished painters and sculptors as Ben Shahn, Leonard Baskin, Peter Blume, Adolph Gottlieb, Jacob Epstein, Jo Davidson, Chaim Gross, Abraham Walkowitz. There John Garfield began his acting career, Nat Holman coached basketball teams, Arthur Murray learned to dance, David Sarnoff studied English, and Sholem Aleichem discussed Yiddish literature.

The Alliance taught adult immigrants English with the aid of Yiddish-speaking instructors. Some five hundred students attended (while a thousand waited for space), the day workers going at night, the night workers going during the day. The immigrants of whatever age were saturated with the English language, so that in a short time the Yiddish brought from Eastern Europe was liberally sprinkled with English words and phrases.

The Friday-evening forums conducted at the Alliance were famous for the quality of the speakers and the liveliness of the discussion. One winter, for instance, the series dealt almost entirely with labor issues—trade unions, strikes, arbitration, cooperation versus competition.

One of the favorite teachers at the Alliance was a non-Jew, Edward King. Born in Massachusetts in 1848, King started as a reporter and editor and then poured his talents and energy into the labor movement and the fight for civil liberties. Deeply sympathetic with the ghetto Jews, he wrote one of the best novels on Lower East Side life (*Joseph Zalmonah*). He taught history at the Alliance and exerted a strong influence on the intellectual growth of the newcomers. Abraham Cahan, his close friend, said that King "became a kind of patriarchal uncle in our little world of Russian-Jewish immigrants."

How a man like King could affect the immigrants whose

lives he touched is depicted in the memoirs of Maurice Hindus. As a youngster, Hindus wandered by chance into one of King's evening lectures. He left this impression of the man:

> *On a small platform beside a stand piled with books, some of them open, stood a short stocky man with a rolling abdomen and a lofty forehead. He wore glasses, and his eyes were overhung by brows as massive and gray as his mustache. He spoke with a fluency, a fervor that held his audience entranced. So many were the learned words he used that I understood only a small part of what he was saying. Yet I too found myself immersed in the lecture. The warmth of the man, the melodiousness of his voice, the magnificence of his diction stirred me. Sweat shone on his brow, and he frequently wiped it with a handkerchief. On and on he spoke, earnestly, thoughtfully, and neither he nor his audience showed the least fatigue. The thrill of hearing him was all the greater because of my identification of words that I had learned from the dictionary and my study book, but that I had never used and never had heard anyone else use.*

When the lecture was over, Hindus stayed for the discussion and was noticed by King after most of the audience had left. "Reaching out his hand, he greeted me with a hearty handshake and a word of welcome. Then I knew that, so far as he was concerned, my knee pants did not matter." He asked the boy a few questions about himself. Hindus said his hardest job was to master English. King suggested the better way was not to memorize words out of a dictionary and textbook but to start reading a novel that would be easier to understand and more interesting to follow. He advised Hindus to jot down words he didn't know and after finishing a page look them up in a dictionary, write out their definitions, and memorize them. Then he was to reread the page, and if he knew all the words, go on in the same way to the next page and the next till he finished the book.

Hindus came back the next week and King gave him George Eliot's *Adam Bede* to start with. Hindus followed his advice, and to his immense joy his knowledge of the language grew very rapidly. Visiting King in his small apartment on the Lower East Side, Hindus found it overflowing with books. They cluttered the rooms and hallway and when King's pupils dropped by he would pull some out and talk fascinatingly about the joy of collecting them and reading them. It was a life centered on his books and his students, a life that gave life to generations of immigrants.

Every city the immigrants poured into had its version of an Educational Alliance. In Boston it was Hale House, located on Garland Street in the center of the slum where Mary Antin lived. In her *Promised Land* she tells how Hale House molded the children on the street corners into "noble men and women." To her the settlement was the lighthouse which guided the immigrants through "the perilous torrents of tenement life." Its Natural History Club, through its meetings and frequent field trips to woods and shore, made her into an enthusiastic amateur naturalist.

Hull-House on Chicago's Halsted Street, founded in 1889, became perhaps the best-known example of the settlement movement in America. The settlement workers—Jane Addams, Ellen Starr, Florence Kelley, Alice Hamilton—wanted more meaningful lives for those who lived in the city's poverty. Instead of doing traditional charity work from a safe distance, they went to live among the poor. They soon realized they could never transform the slums without reforming the city, the state, the nation—in fact, the whole social and political fabric of America. In spite of their intense commitment, they often failed to make large or lasting improvement in immigrant life. But they did point to a dynamic current of change, and they succeeded in helping many individual immigrants, especially those ambitious to break free of slum and sweatshop.

One of those who came to Hull-House was Philip Davis, a Jewish immigrant from Russia. He called the settlement his "university of good will, good English, good citizenship." After study at the University of Chicago and Harvard, he became himself a settlement worker and an author. In his autobiography he said this of the settlement's leader:

> *Jane Addams had the happy faculty of liking people of diverse backgrounds. Unlike critics of the immigrants of that day, she encouraged us to build proudly on what was most valuable in our heritage. I remember her listening sympathetically to the account of my boyhood in Motol, of my aunt Weizmann, my little village, and the wedding ceremony. Through such personal conversations with her neighbors on Halsted Street (with Greeks, Italians, Poles, Russians, and many others) she acquired an impressive knowledge of old-world cultures transplanted in part to this nation.*

To encourage pride in national heritage, Hull-House created a theater where the immigrants could present plays in their native tongues. Greeks, Poles, Lithuanians, Russians took great pleasure in this opportunity to educate the ignorant Americans. By 1900 the settlement had its own theater group, the Hull-House Players, which earned national recognition for its professional quality. Typical of its achievement was the production of plays written by immigrants. Hilda Satt, who came from the Warsaw ghetto to Chicago in the 1890s, began working in a factory at thirteen, and had her first play, dealing with working-class life, presented at Hull-House.

The settlement houses were but one example of Jews helping Jews in a time of need. The *mitzva*—the doing of a good deed—was carried out in dozens of different ways. The old charitable societies, founded in the mid-nineteenth

A singing class at Chicago's famous settlement, Hull-House

century, multiplied their clients. But many new organizations were formed under the pressure of the mass influx. They tended to become more specialized, more sophisticated. At first they helped the immigrants with food, lodging, medical services, and jobs, following no general plan, overlapping in function and control, sometimes confused and inefficient. Until, in the early 1900s, the Hebrew Immigrant Aid Society integrated and centralized the work of receiving the newcomers and offering them assistance.

Special responsibility for immigrant women was assumed by the National Council of Jewish Women. It began with a small refuge on Orchard Street "to keep single girls from the hands of the white slavers." Located near a district where prostitution flourished, the refuge helped the young women find jobs and housed them until they could support themselves.

Gradually the immigrant-aid groups learned to unite their fund raising, to substitute professionals for volunteer help, and to plan and spend by "scientific" design. But the immigrants didn't wait to be helped. They resented having nothing to say about the policy of institutions trying to help them. They were angry when their customs, their habits, even their religion, were put down by the kind ladies and gentlemen doing the volunteer work. They feared the wedge being driven between themselves and their children. Falling back upon their own resources, they turned first to their home-town groups—*landsmanshaft* made up of Jews from the same village or neighborhood in the old country. They aided each other through medical, unemployment, and strike insurance. They provided interest-free loans, sick benefits and disability payments, funeral costs and burial plots. This was better, they felt—taking part in the mutual aid of your own group rather than accepting charitable patronage. Just as important was the deep need to join with your friends in maintaining some connection with the old country, with the life of the past. They were trying to make the *landsmanshaft* take the place of the *shtetl.*

In the Old World the *shul,* the synagogue, had been the center of Jewish communal life. But in America the synagogues multiplied in chaotic fashion. Religion was no longer so important in bonding Jews together. The divisive pressures of big-city living led the immigrants to seek outside the synagogue for the satisfaction of social needs. So the religious societies that had once provided social benefits too gave way to a variety of groups, large and small, such as the *landsmanshaft.* Hundreds of them in New York and other cities reached into almost every immigrant home. In nearly every household was the *pushke,* the little collection box to hold the pennies destined for scores of charitable causes.

The self-help groups founded their own orphanages, hospitals, and homes for the elderly. Only this way could they be sure of a kosher diet and the warm Jewish atmosphere they desired. They organized societies for helping widows, children, prisoners, unwed mothers, the deaf, the blind, the tubercular, the retarded, the crippled.

It didn't take long to see how much better it would be if these random efforts were pulled together. The Federation of Jewish Philanthropies became the means for coordinating all such agencies. The American Jewish Committee was formed in defense of Jewish interests here and overseas. When World War I broke out, the American Jewish Joint Distribution Committee was shaped out of existing organizations to carry on relief work in Europe. As the war came to an end, the American Jewish Congress was organized to work for the establishment of a Jewish national home in Palestine and for the defense of the civil rights of Jews everywhere.

15 | My Parents Don't Understand

In the passage from the culture of Eastern Europe to the broader stream of American modernity, much that was Jewish was often thrown overboard. The major centers of Jewish life—the home, the synagogue, and the school—were gradually deserted.

"I want to forget," said Mary Antin, "sometimes I long to forget. . . . It is painful to be consciously of two worlds. The Wandering Jew in me seeks forgetfulness." It was easy to Americanize her name and her clothes, harder to drop Yiddish and master English, but she managed to do that and quickly too, proud that she even learned "to think in English without an accent."

But what could she do about her father? That middle-aged man from Polotzk—he was too obviously Eastern European and Jewish to keep up with his Mashke-called-Mary. In spite of how he tried, he would always, she said, be "hindered by a natural inability to acquire the English language." He was tied to the monumental past, but not Mary. "I am the youngest of America's children," she said. Polotzk was gone forever.

For the freedom to be an individual, the Jewish immigrants risked the dissolution of their group. Everything which America might find foreign they must decide whether to discard. Mary Antin moved speedily to adopt the American way of life. But no one forced her to. In America the process of making your way into the broader community was as fast or as slow as you chose to move. If you liked, you could remain in the ghetto until you died. This was a big country, with room for Lower East Sides in whatever city you picked to live.

Inevitably the movement toward assimilation led to conflict between the immigrants and their American-born children. When the older generation tried to keep elements of their native culture it often made the children ashamed of their parents. Children need a sense of security and a feeling of acceptance if they are to enjoy healthy emotional growth. The transplanted immigrant parents had a degree of both security and acceptance in their relations with immigrants of their own kind among whom they usually lived in the new country. But their children grew up with bilingual and bicultural conflicts at home, in the school, and on the playground. They lacked their parents' memories of the old country to give them rootedness and security and a sense of their own value. And if they turned to their parents with questions about the new country, the answer was often, "I don't know."

Worse, whatever marked the child's parents as foreign labeled them as inferior. To win acceptance the child had to make himself into an "American." It meant rebellion against parental authority; and often too it meant contempt for one's own ethnic identity. Everything that was Jewish (or Italian or Polish or Armenian or Greek or . . .) was rejected. Evelyn W. Hersey, who studied the American-born children of immigrant parents, concluded, "I have come to believe that this pervasive feeling of rejection of 'foreignness' is felt by all second-generation young people no matter how secure and adequate they seem."

The influence of everything American was irresistible. The immigrants found themselves suddenly the parents of *American* children. They felt astonishment, shock, pride, regret, but what could they do about it? They were helpless in the face of the glorification of America and the passionate desire of children to be exactly like their schoolmates.

Jim was the sixteen-year-old son of Jewish immigrants who lived in a California neighborhood mostly of non-Jews. Interviewed in *Survey* magazine, he talked of his conflicts with his parents.

I don't like to bring my American friends around. They were born here and so were their parents. My mother speaks "English" to them, and they make fun of her. When I ask her to leave them alone she says: "They are only goyim [Gentiles], ain't I good enough to entertain them?" Sure, she "entertains" them—at my expense. My father won't allow us to play ball on the lot. He says it's a waste of time and a disgrace to make such a lot of noise over nothing. He was raised in Poland. But then he don't believe in sweatshops either, but has never been anything but a cutter in a sweatshop. It's awfully embarrassing to bring any American friends to the house. . . .

My parents don't believe in beaches and never go swimming. I don't like to stay home, and my parents don't understand what boys need, and they expect me to be old-fashioned and go to shul.

I have never taken very much stock in religion. I don't

*see any sense in it. Our Sabbath begins Friday at sunset,
but my father works in the shop all day Saturday. Oh, he
sighs and hopes to be in the land of the "faithful" before
he dies, but that don't help him any. I don't see why a
faithful people should suffer and be laughed at like we
are. My parents nag me to go to shul on holidays. They
make many sacrifices to keep their traditions, but they
don't mean anything much in my life. . . . That's just
why I don't like to stay home. I don't want to hurt my
parents and I can't follow their advice.*

Few of the Jewish (or other) immigrants escaped the
clash of cultures. Some parents bitterly fought off any
change which might weaken the values they brought with
them. Others, seeing it was a losing battle, resigned themselves to maintaining their culture for themselves while
tolerating their children's adoption of new beliefs and
behavior. A third group, determined to keep close bonds
with their children, gave up their own culture and plunged
into Americanization themselves. ("If you can't lick 'em,
join 'em.")

The Jewish education centers—the *cheder* and the
Hebrew school—were another source of conflict between
parents and children. The immigrant generation started
them, but the American-born generation turned away from
them. While the parents gave wholehearted support to
the public schools, they wanted their children to get a
Jewish education as well. That meant schooling in the
Torah and the Talmud. Here it had to be confined to
hours outside the public-school sessions.

All over the Lower East Side, *cheders* sprang up to offer
Jewish tutoring. They were schools privately owned and

An elementary religious school—a *cheder*—on the Lower East Side

operated by individual *rebbes* (teachers), many of them ill prepared. It was learning by slapping. The pupils were crowded into a single small room, often in a cellar. Fees were fifty cents to a dollar a month.

Teachers and *cheder* are sketched by Henry Roth in his novel of East Side childhood, *Call It Sleep*.

> *He was not at all like the teachers at school. . . . He appeared old and was certainly untidy. He wore soft leather shoes like house-slippers, that had no place for either laces or buttons. His trousers were baggy and stained, a great area of striped and crumpled shirt intervened between his belt and his bulging vest. The knot of his tie, which was nearer one ear than the other, hung away from his soiled collar. What features were visible were large and had an oily gleam. Beneath his skull-cap, his black hair was closely cropped. Though full of misgivings about his future relations with the rabbi, David felt that he must accept his fate. Was it not his father's decree that he attend a cheder? . . .*
>
> *David sat down, and the rabbi walked back to his seat beside the window. Instead of sitting down, however, he reached under his chair, and bringing out a short-thonged cat-o'-nine-tails, struck the table loudly with the butt-end and pronounced in a menacing voice: "Let there be a hush among you!" And a scared silence instantly locking all mouths, he seated himself. He then picked up a little stick lying on the table and pointed to the book, whereupon a boy sitting next to him began droning out sounds in a strange and secret tongue.*

Other schools—the Talmud Torahs—were supported by the community. They were designed to give an elementary Jewish education to both boys and girls, rich or poor. There were a variety of kinds, arising from the different religious and social trends struggling for supremacy within the Jewish community. But they diminished in numbers as parents and children alike grew unwilling to see so much time given to what seemed to matter less and less. The schools did not produce students really at home in the Hebrew language and familiar with its scriptures and literature. And what use was Jewish education in an American society where religion played no central role?

Rather than require children to attend two separate schools—the public and the Jewish—some parents organized all-day schools in which the curriculum was divided between Jewish studies and general studies. These ran from kindergarten through high school and were supported by tuition fees and contributions.

The Jewish religious schools failed to attract or keep more than a fraction of the immigrants' children. "Jewishness, Hebrew learning, and tradition," as Azriel Eisenberg pointed out, "were equated with foreignness, squalor, and boredom, and thus came to be regarded with contempt and antagonism."

It was the same with youthful attendance at the synagogue. These multiplied rapidly as the Eastern European immigration rose. In 1880 there were 270 in New York. By 1916 the number was 1,900. But most of the congregations were small. Only ten Jews are needed to form a congregation and they are free to worship as they desire. Jews from one *shtetl* or neighborhood in the old country (*landsleit* they were called) converted stores or tenement flats into their own tiny houses of worship. The religion that had governed their lives from birth was still vital to them. But much less so to their children.

Trying to explain this to a New York *Tribune* reporter in

1903, the head of the Educational Alliance, Dr. David Blaustein, underscored the enormous difference between the role of the synagogue in Czarist Russia and its role in the United States.

> *The Jew [in the old country] is never interfered with in his religious observances. He simply loses, on account of them, all civic and economic rights. He pays for his religious liberty with the latter. His church has infinitely greater power and importance in Russia than in America. The rabbi keeps all the vital statistics. The rabbi marries and divorces. The rabbi has charge of all education. He also acts as a court in both civil and criminal cases. . . . At every turn of the road the Jew's religion is recognized. He is taxed as a Jew, enlisted as a Jew. . . . You can imagine the confusion in the immigrant's mind when he reaches America. He finds his church of no account whatever. No one cares what church he belongs to or whether he belongs to any church or not. The state delegates no rights or powers to the church. All that is asked is whether he is an American or not. . . . In place of finding the congregation all powerful and all embracing, he finds when he joins a congregation that he has simply joined a liberal society . . . a mutual benefit society . . . a clubroom where the men meet to talk over old times, read letters from home, discuss politics . . . or study the Talmud. . . . Religious services are also held, with one of their number, not necessarily an ordained rabbi, acting as leader.*

Still, there was a loyalty to modern Jewish spiritual values which many immigrants did not want to give up. Resisting the American pressure for total assimilation, they wanted to see Jewish group life strengthened. They opposed the early Jewish socialists who envisioned a society in which all national differences would be erased. They believed nationalism could be a creative force for spiritual and cultural betterment. Intellectuals like Chaim Zhitlowsky (1865–1943) exerted a powerful influence campaigning for the opening of Jewish secular schools to teach modern Jewish culture centered on the Yiddish language. This, they believed, would help bind Jews together so that they could continue creatively as a people.

The Labor Zionists were the first to open such a school, in 1910. Within a few years there were two other programs following the secularist trend in Jewish education—the Workmen's Circle schools and the Sholem Aleichem schools. Eventually it was realized that teaching the Jewish religion "from a cultural historical standpoint" was necessary to explain to children why Jews are what they are. All three types of schools came to recognize Bar Mitzvah and to celebrate Jewish holidays in both their childhood and adult-education programs.

With the stress shifting from religious to secular learning, the model for the young to pattern their lives upon was no longer the rabbi or the Talmudist but the professional or the scholar.

But before the flight from the ghetto turned into a stampede, there was an extraordinary time when a secular Jewish culture flourished in America.

16 | Cahan and the Cafés

After generations of censorship, what must it feel like to know sudden freedom to speak, write, assemble, organize, think as you please? How different America was from the Czarist prison house! The immigrant Jews rushed to exercise their new-found right of expression. Liberated journalists, pamphleteers, orators, poets, novelists, dramatists, actors exploded with an energy and intelligence that astounded the outside world.

One of the newcomers who landed at the beginning of the mass immigration was Abraham Cahan. When he arrived in 1882, the Yiddish-speaking population was about a quarter million. The *shul* was their only institution. There was no Jewish press, no literature, no theater, no labor movement, no political party. Cahan's would be the most powerful hand in the shaping of the cultural life of the immigrant community.

Cahan was born in 1860 in a Lithuanian *shtetl*, the only child of a poor family which moved to Vilna before he was six. He studied at a yeshiva, went to a government school, began reading Russian writers, and lost his faith in Judaism. While working as a Jewish teacher he joined the revolutionary underground plotting to overthrow czarism. When Alexander II was assassinated in 1881 he escaped arrest and fled to the United States. He learned English quickly and began teaching it to immigrants. Plunging into New York's radical movement, he became a noted speaker, giving the first lectures in Yiddish on socialism. Soon he was reporting in English for the New York newspapers while editing and writing for the Yiddish socialist press at the same time. In 1897 he helped found the Jewish socialist daily, the *Forward* (*Forverts*), but soon left it to work in English as a reporter for the New York daily press. He published short stories and novels in English which dealt with immigrant life in the tenements and sweatshops of the Lower East Side. He became the friend of men like the muckraking reporter Lincoln Steffens and the novelist William Dean Howells. In 1902 he returned to the *Forward*, which he edited with absolute control for almost fifty years.

His plan was to put out a paper for the Jewish immigrant masses, not just for the small group of socialists at whom the Yiddish press usually aimed. His target was an audience unfamiliar with a daily paper. (There had been no Yiddish daily in Russia.) To arouse interest he adapted the methods of the big New York papers—sensational news stories topped by screaming headlines, reader contests, features on love and sex. But at the same time he meant to hang on to the Jewish workers who were passionately involved in labor and socialist activity. For them he published articles by the leading European socialists, novels by such men as Sholem Asch and I. J. Singer, and poems by dozens of Yiddish writers.

If numbers are proof, Cahan succeeded. He built the

Forward from a circulation of 6,000 in 1902 to a peak of 250,000 in the late 1920s. During the earlier years the *Forward* was a great force for organizing the Jewish trade unions and the Socialist Party. The paper wrote about the need to organize, to fight for higher wages and lower hours, for decent treatment by the bosses, for a new and better social system. At the same time Cahan led the paper in a campaign to speed the Americanization of his readers. He taught the largely uneducated masses of the pre-1905 migration their cultural ABCs. But, his critics said, he never carried them beyond. He kept to the elementary level of Anglo-Saxon manners and mores, with editorials on how to use a handkerchief instead of the sleeve or how to set a table properly. He showed a great talent for popularization, making the contents of the *Forward* appealing to the non-socialist immigrants he was trying to bring closer to the movement.

One of his best-read innovations was "Das Bintel Brief" ("A Sheaf of Letters"), a daily feature started in 1906. It gave readers a chance to express themselves through letters to the paper. A flood of mail began to come in daily, readers opening their hearts to others, describing their personal problems, seeking advice, approval, consolation. It was a timely outlet for a mass of immigrants deeply troubled by the tensions of a new life, so vastly different in custom and code from what they had lived by in the old country. There they could take their troubles to the rabbi. Here they could seek help from the editor. They wrote about poverty, hunger, sickness, about love and divorce, about joblessness, intermarriage, loss of faith in Judaism, or on socialism, about parents versus children. . . . Often the questions raised were thrown open for public discussion and readers sent in their opinions. Women became the closest followers of "Das Bintel Brief" and the most frequent contributors.

As editor, Cahan insisted on getting a "Yiddish Yiddish" from his writers. He rejected the stilted form of Germanized Yiddish in favor of a plain Yiddish the ordinary Jews spoke at home and at work. He encouraged his writers to follow the general custom of incorporating incorrectly pronounced English words into their Yiddish articles, thus opening himself to the charge of corrupting the language. Yiddish writers who loved their language attacked Cahan for spitting on it. He was promoting *shund*, they said, meaning he was serving up a cheap mixture of vulgarity and sentimentality. Cahan's defense was that it worked: his readers liked the penny paper—circulation, advertising, and profits kept rising. One of his colleagues, Melech Epstein, said that while Cahan built the *Forward* into a powerful medium, he learned too much from William Randolph Hearst.

The *Forward*, while the leading Yiddish daily, was only one of nearly a hundred Jewish papers born between 1885 and 1900. In New York alone, about twenty Yiddish dailies came to life in the great immigration period. "The Yiddish press," says one of its critics, Lucy Dawidowicz, "had a violent and extremist tone, whether politically conservative and Orthodox or radical and antireligious. The irresponsible tone, with slashing accusations directed against government, capital, Jewish institutions, or competing papers, was due partly to the license spawned by American freedom, and partly to the lessons learned from the yellow journalism that William Randolph Hearst was then cultivating."

Whatever its weaknesses, this was the press that nourished the migrating Jewish millions in their own language. And that language? Harry Roskolenko defines it.

> *Yiddish was a language of journalism that was indeed new to America but old, for those who could read, in Eastern Europe. There it had come into its own as a wanderer's speech, picking up, after its basic "German," words in Russian, Polish, Romanian, Hungarian—and the related words and sounds that came with the borrowings of many tongues. Each country had added special words or words had been altered by accents, to merge with the Jewish created during the Middle Ages—and to add confusion as well as cohesion to East Broadway's variegated readers of Yiddish. On the wide streets were editors, satirists, playwrights, novelists—and working journalists, often the same people. A poet, too, was always a journalist—in order to make some sort of living, when he was not, too often, working in a factory. . . . No matter what a man did, it was done with accents, flavors, and gusto in his speech. It was a Yiddish of many variations and humor that one Jew spoke to another, and what they said dealt with what they did.*

Among the other prominent Jewish papers was *The Day*, directed to a more literary and scholarly audience, and with an English section to help integration along. It was Democratic and Zionist, and purist in its approach to Yiddish. The *Morning Journal* was both Republican and Orthodox. For the anarchists there was *Der Freie Arbeiter Stimme* (*The Free Worker's Voice*), which was still going in the early 1970s, eighty years after its birth. And for the Communists there was the *Freiheit*, founded in 1922. Assessing them as a group, Judd Teller concluded, "The caliber of their serious material surpassed anything that the metropolitan press has ever offered. . . ." Morris R. Cohen, too, thought the Yiddish press did more than the English press for the education of its readers. "It tried to give its readers something of enduring and substantial value. . . . The Yiddish press has prepared millions of Jewish people to take a worthy part in American civilization while also promoting the natural self-respect to which Jews are entitled because of their character and history."

East Broadway was where most of the Yiddish papers were published in those years. The journalists met in the lunchrooms and over herring, bread, and tea damned one another's pieces, politics, and papers. Their work was often sentimental and primitive, its main impulse to evoke tears. But when Yiddish was not crying, said Roskolenko, who used to peddle the papers, it could reach the level of the best world press.

The one-block triangle where East Broadway, Canal, and Division streets met was called Rutgers Square. At the turn of the century it became for the Lower East Side what the Piazza San Marco was for Venice or St. Stephen's Platz for Vienna. S. L. Blumenson, who knew it in those years, recalls what it was like.

> During the day Rutgers Square was a quiet business district, but with the coming of darkness it erupted "kultur" like an active volcano: religion and atheism, free love and vegetarianism, politics and ideologies. But in peace. The presence of our neighbor, Thomas Mulvaney, and the "billy" in his belt, gave kapuler untzuherenes (tactful hints) that culture would not be disturbed.

Nearby in a basement was the café called Zum Essex, whose owner (and cook) was Sigmund Manilescu, a dignified Rumanian Jew. There the feuding factionalists of the worlds of politics and art adjourned from the street corners or theaters to continue their disputes.

The Zum Essex was famous for its lavish cuisine. Sigmund served a five-course dinner (supper) consisting of soup, meat, potato, stewed prunes, and all the pumpernickel one could eat, for the price of twelve cents. (To Litvaks he made a concession: he served herring and onion instead of soup.) In addition, any steady customer could come in any time for a free glass of seltzer. On Friday night, the Sabbath meal, he added generous portions of gefilte fish, with strong horseradish flavored with beet juice. Sigmund was as proud of his horseradish as a French chef is of his special salad dressing. A moment's pause for soda water. It was fizzing seltzer flavored with a dollop of syrup, and in those days it cost a penny a glass. The favorite flavors were vanilla, chocolate, strawberry, raspberry, lemon and mint, shelved in colored bottles to tempt the eye. For two cents the glass was a bit bigger and the syrup a bit richer. But who had two cents?

On the south side of East Broadway was the meeting place of the Brotherly Beneficial and Kultur Society.

Its purpose was to help needy brothers in distress and to spread Kultur through lectures (pronounced "lektzyes"), discussions and forlezungen (readings). During the business part of the meetings the members addressed each other with the title of bruder (brother); during political discussions as genosse (comrade); during

cultural debate as kolege *(colleague), with the hard "g."*
It was considered an insult to be called bruder *or* genosse
when engaged in cultural pursuits. . . .

Once a week, on Friday nights, there were popular
lectures by members of the unemployed pool of lec-
turers. The persecutions in Russia had driven many writ-
ers, intellectuals, and students into exile, and some by
way of Germany and Paris and London came to the East
Side seeking employment. Among these were names like
Feigenbaum, Zametkin, Winchevsky, Girizansky, Kats,
Selivokits, Philip Krantz, Jacob Magidoff, Hermalin,
Kobrin, Zevin, and later Chaim Zhitlowsky and many
others who were to become well-known journalists and
authors.

An actor and artist called Kolege Lebel, a member of the
Kultur committee, had a special contribution to make.
Blumenson, his second cousin, describes what it was.

Lebel was an exponent of the Little Theater move-
ment and directed a little theater group made up of
some of the members of the Society and their girl
friends. He favored such plays as Der Yiddisher Kenig
Lear, Der Yiddisher Hamlet, Der Yiddisher Rober fun
Schiller, Di Yiddishe Medea, Di Yiddishe Veber fun
Hauptmann, Di Yiddishe Verzunkene Glocke, Got,
Mensh un Teufel *by Jacob Gordin, and most of all,*
The Bells *by Emile Erekmann. Nice light plays, as you*
can see. Lebel's whole spare time was devoted to the
theater. . . .

Lebel was also in great demand by many East Side
radical organizations for staging "lebedige pikches,"

dramatic clusters of living statues, at their annual balls. . . . At all these joyous occasions half the space was usually occupied with the posturings of Kolege Lebel's groups. In one corner five or six miners were dying of silicosis, and their wives and small children, faces full of talcum powder, were starving to death. Another group featured consumptive garment workers coughing away over their sewing machines, while a boss with an artificially bloated stomach stood over them with a whip. Lebel's artistic groupings were greatly enjoyed by everyone and were praised in the radical press.

On the north side of East Broadway was the meeting place of the Kolege's hated rivals, the youthful anarchists of the Pioneers of Freedom. "Most of them were in their teens," said Blumenson, "newly arrived from the small towns and villages of Russia and Galicia and Poland, where they had been compelled to follow small-town *derech eretz* (conventions) and the strict rules of Orthodoxy. Now they were behaving like young colts let out to pasture for the first time." They loved to sing and dance, and to welcome arriving exiles with banquets. The feasts, prepared by the Zum Essex for nine cents a guest, were topped off by fizzing seltzer toasts to the honored guest and hymns to the coming revolution. To spite God, the anarchists sometimes held their celebrations in their own clubrooms, where "they served ham sandwiches, smearing loads of sharp mustard to kill the taste, and tea *with milk*." It shocked the Orthodox on the East Side, who called such outrageous affairs *chazer* (pig) parties.

The real intellectual comrades, says Blumenson, met on Norfolk Street in Sachs' Café.

There the "cream" of the radikalen *gathered nightly, and over Mrs. Sachs's fine coffee and famous cheesecake discussed the problems and philosophies of the day. Unlike the* genessen *in Herrick's Café, there was no gesticulation or noisy argument. These were mannerly,* gemuetliche *intellectuals, exiles and martyrs of world revolution, graduates of many famous universities.*

At one table would be Comrade Solataroff, well-known lecturer and exponent of world revolution. Beside him Comrade Kats, editor of Die Freie Gezelshaft, *the Yiddish anarchist weekly opposing the policies of editor Yanofsky of the* Freie Arbeiter Stimme. . . . *At Comrade Yanofsky's table sat the "Poet of Revolt," Edelstadt, the "Yiddisher François Villon," reciting his latest epic to a fascinated audience. There was "Grandpa" Net-*

YIVO *Institute for Jewish Research*

An artist's sketch of one of the East Side cafés where politics and culture mixed with tea, schnapps, and seltzer

ter, a bearded patriarch, a great Talmudist, who in his old age repudiated Orthodoxy and joined the Comrades. With him was his daughter, Chaverte (fem: chaver, comrade) Netter, young and good-looking and devoted to the holy cause. At other tables were slummers, members of the English-language press looking for local color, and occasionally members of the Bomb Squad, in very evident disguise.

There were cafés of all kinds, some of them only smelly saloons in damp and dirty cellars where the beer, the kvass, and the schnapps tasted sour. There were cafés for domino players where the game was everything and cafés for newspaper readers where men hid behind the pages and slurped tea from saucers while they groaned over the news from the old country. Above all, the cafés were forums for argumentative Jews, and there was never a shortage of these. Harry Roskolenko heard them all as he peddled his papers inside.

The talkers were men of extraordinary abilities—as talkers. Talk was the major art of the cafés with these aristocrats of rhetoric, the bringers of useless data, as they competed with their compote-quotes about all things of value. In this free arena, the circus without measure, it was the claque that each man had that denoted the worth of the speaker-orator-lecturer-statesman-schnorrer. It was private meandering, public pontificating—and no decisions; for the talk went on for weeks or until one speaker suddenly decided that the dead end was truly dead. Running out of his audience, he moved to another café. There he built another circus with newer spectators, philosophers—and kibitzers, for they could not always be told apart easily. . . .

Ideas about God, the synagogue, the union, inter-meshed. It was difficult, then, for me to see how men could be two things—like Zionist-anarchists; or Zionists who were also atheists; or socialists who were Zionists and atheists. It was like a chess game—with no rules. . . . Who was not at least two or three separate spiritual and physical entities on the Lower East Side? My father managed socialism, Orthodoxy and Zionism, quite easily, and so did the kibitzers and the serious.

17 | Actors and Poets

The Yiddish theater rivaled the Yiddish press in popular appeal. The actors were even greater folk heroes than the journalists. For cold print could hardly match the living stage in evoking an electric response from the Jewish immigrants. The origins of the Yiddish theater are traced back to the traditional Purim play, which dramatized annually the Book of Esther. The religious occasion was the only time that Eastern European Jews could enjoy public entertainment. In the mid-nineteenth century the rigid ban on secular drama relaxed in Rumania, where Yiddish singers and instrumentalists of Hasidic background began to entertain in the cafés of the cities. Hasidic folk material was gradually worked up into skits which framed the songs.

The first playwright was Abraham Goldfaden, a Russian Jew who became a teacher and wrote poems and songs in Hebrew and Yiddish. Unable to support his family, he went into business, failed, and then tried journalism, moving to Rumania to edit a paper. Encouraged by a Yiddish café entertainer who sang his songs, he began in 1876 to write musical plays for his own traveling theatrical troupe.

Other companies arose, sustained by a Jewish audience hungry for this kind of entertainment. In 1879 Goldfaden took his troupe touring in southern Russia, recruiting new actors on the road. Many of them were to achieve stardom later on East Side stages.

The few Yiddish playwrights limited themselves at first to domestic comedy. Then they turned to Jewish folk material and Biblical sources, converting them into historical operettas. Their next step was to adapt plays on Jewish themes written by Gentiles, putting them into Yiddish. In 1883 the growth of the infant art was suddenly choked off by the Czar; he issued a ban on all Yiddish theater in Russia. The fledgling dramatists and actors had to go abroad to start new theaters. Some went to Germany, to England, to Rumania; one group, with Joseph Lateiner as playwright, headed for America. In 1884 the company gave its first performance in New York, on East Fourth Street, and later established the Oriental Theater on the Bowery. (Two years earlier a group of amateurs, composed chiefly of the Thomashefsky family from Kiev, had performed briefly on the Bowery.)

By the turn of the century there were three major Yiddish theaters flourishing on the Bowery, employing some eighty professional actors who performed the works of about a dozen prolific playwrights. (The combined output of three of them ran to over three hundred plays.) Goldfaden's charming folk operas—*Shmendrik* and *The Two Kuni-Lemels*—remained a staple of the repertory, but other writers had taken over the creation of new material. Two of them, Lateiner and Moshe Horowitz, "together brought Yiddish theater to a new low," as Ronald Sanders put it. Horowitz, who dominated the Windsor Theater, wrote more than 160 plays, largely romantic and inaccurate adaptations of Jewish history. They were clumsy, conventional melodramas, "full of historical plunder," as one critic charged. One reason for the superabundance and low quality was the short run most plays had. They rarely went over twelve performances and often had only three or four. The dramatists sold their rights for as little as $25 to $85. The audience, which had never seen professional theater in the old country, was an easy victim of trash.

The most favored playwright of the Yiddish audiences for some time was Joseph Lateiner. As feverish a writer as Horowitz, he ground out over one hundred plays, "no one of which," commented Hutchins Hapgood, "has form or ideas." They were a mishmash of melodrama and vaudeville—exactly what, Lateiner insisted, his audience wanted. Hapgood, who went to see them, said they were "the very spirit of formlessness—burlesque, popularly vulgar jokes, flat heroism combining about the flimsiest dramatic structure." To intellectual critics Lateiner was a businessman, not an artist. He often wrote directly for the star of his company at the Thalia—Boris Thomashefsky (1868–1939). Boris, "young, fat, with curling black hair, languorous eyes . . . was thought very beautiful by the girls of the ghetto," said Hapgood. With Jacob P. Adler (1855–1926) and David Kessler (1860–1920) Boris shared the heights of popularity in that era.

The three Yiddish theaters they performed in expressed the world of the Lower East Side. The performances drew the entire community, wrote Hapgood.

Into these three buildings crowd the Jews of all the ghetto classes, the sweatshop woman with her baby, the day laborer, the small Hester Street shopkeeper, the Rus-sian-Jewish anarchist and socialist, the ghetto rabbi and scholar, the poet, the journalist. The poor and ignorant are in the great majority, but the learned, the intellec-tual, and the progressive are also represented, and here, as elsewhere, exert a more than numerically propor-tionate influence on the character of the theatrical pro-ductions, which, nevertheless, remain essentially popu-lar. The socialists and the literati create the demand that forces into the mass of vaudeville, light opera and his-torical and melodramatic plays a more serious art ele-ment, a simple transcript from life or the theatric presen-tation of a ghetto problem. But this more serious ele-ment is so saturated with the simple manners, humor, and pathos of the life of the poor Jews that it is seldom above the heartfelt understanding of the crowd.

On the first four weekdays the theaters were sold out to clubs, lodges, and unions for benefit performances. It was the beginning of the theater-party system. On weekends— Friday, Saturday, and Sunday nights—the tickets were bought directly by playgoers at twenty-five cents to a dollar.

On these nights the theater presents a peculiarly pic-turesque sight. Poor workingmen and women with their babies of all ages fill the theater. Great enthusiasm is manifested, sincere laughter and tears accompany the sincere acting on the stage. Peddlers of soda water, candy, of fantastic gewgaws of many kinds, mix freely with the audience between the acts. Conversation during the play is received with strenuous hisses, but the falling of the curtain is the signal for groups of friends to get together and gossip about the play or the affairs of the week.

The break with the Horowitz-Lateiner brand of theater came through Jacob Gordin. Gordin, born in the Ukraine in 1853, rejected both Orthodoxy and Jewish nationalism when a youth. He married and became editor of a small Russian paper seeking to bring "light, education, and hope" to the Jewish people. In 1891 he came to New York with his wife and eight children. He wrote his first literary sketches in Yiddish for the press, using much dialogue. A meeting with the actor Jacob Adler spurred him to try his hand at playwriting. His first effort, *Siberia*, was in the tragic vein of Russian realism which the East Side intellectuals so admired. Abraham Cahan praised the play as a

YIVO *Institute for Jewish Research*

Stars of the Yiddish theater in the 1890s: (*left to right*) David Kessler, Max Abramovitch, Rudolph Marx, Sigmund Mogulesco, Sigmund Feinman, and Jacob Adler

departure from the secondhand melodrama and predicted it would "bring about a complete revolution on the Yiddish stage." Gordin's next play was *The Pogrom*. He went on to write problem plays about ghetto life, voicing the rebellion against poverty and injustice which brought passionate applause from the socialists in the audience. His play *The Beggar of Odessa* pitted rich villains against the noble poor. In *Vogele* the poor Jews satirized the rich Jews. *Mirele Efros* portrayed Jewish life in old Russia. *Minna* was a drama about a Yiddish Nora in an East Side Doll's House. Gordin's *Jewish King Lear*, adapting Shakespeare to the ghetto, dramatized the painful break between immigrant parents and Americanized children. It was a great success and led Gordin to write more plays based upon the themes and plots of masterpieces of world drama. The note he sounded most frequently was the cry for women's emancipation.

Gordin wrote more than sixty plays, many for Adler, who was the most ardent promoter of serious Yiddish drama. But Kessler and Thomashefsky, too, often performed in Gordin's plays. Sadly, straight realism had a hard time on the Bowery. Even from the actors. They loved to ad-lib dialogue and to improvise whatever action the spirit moved them to try. Gordin had to struggle against them to preserve the integrity of his text. Even so, to win and keep audiences, he sometimes inserted clownish or operatic moments in his work. By the early 1900s he and Adler grew pessimistic about the future of Yiddish drama. They felt commercialism would kill it even before the Americanization of their audiences turned them away from the Yiddish language. But though *shund* persisted, the Yiddish theater experienced a revival during World War I which extended

A scene from the Yiddish Art Theatre's production of Ansky's *The Dybbuk*: Maurice Schwartz (*above*) as the messenger, and Lazar Freed as the Talmudic student

through the 1930s. In 1918 the actor Maurice Schwartz launched the Yiddish Art Theater with a company that included Paul Muni and Jacob Ben-Ami. Plays by Sholem Aleichem, Peretz, Hirschbein, David Pinski, Osip Dimov, Z. Libin, and Leon Kobrin won new audiences for their superior quality. Gordin died in 1909, but his plays, translated into many European languages, are still performed here and abroad.

Was the American theater in any better condition than the Yiddish? Lincoln Steffens thought it worse. He wrote in his autobiography that in those years the best theater in New York City was the Yiddish. Professors of drama used to take their students to see Gordin's plays, likening him to Ibsen (a comparison which hardly stands up today). Still, how many American dramatists were trying to lend aesthetic universality to the daily life around them? In any event, serious Yiddish theater lost ground rapidly when ten-cent vaudeville and the ten-cent movie flooded the East Side.

If Jacob Gordin was considered the great monument of the drama in that pre-World War I era, Morris Rosenfeld is often held up as the peak of Yiddish poetry. "But upon closer examination," says Lucy Dawidowicz, "they appear like Hollywood foam-rubber boulders, an illusion created by distance and accepted as real because of condescending and indulgent literary standards. The Yiddish theater and Yiddish poets like Rosenfeld fascinated outsiders who were captured by the energy and intelligence of the Jewish immigrants. No doubt they felt much like Samuel Johnson about a woman preaching—not that it was done well, but surprised that it was done at all, like a dog walking on its hind legs."

What can be said for that early East Side literature, she

goes on, is that "it testifies to the powerful persistence of folk poetry" among the Yiddish-speaking immigrants.

The tradition of writing for the people goes back to the early nineteenth century. Not art for art's sake, but writing for the ordinary reader was the foundation of authentic Yiddish literature. Out of the Haskalah came a new Jewish literature that functioned in two languages—Hebrew and Yiddish. The early Haskalists scorned Yiddish as the jargon of the ignorant masses, the brand of an exiled people. Yet, when two thirds of the world's Jews spoke not Hebrew but Yiddish, how else could they reach the unenlightened? They were driven to the use of Yiddish.

As the wave of assimilation swept many young people away from Jewish identity, and anti-Semitism peaked in widespread pogroms, Jewish writers began to change their views. The Haskalah "failed to provide us with a philosophy we could live by," said I. L. Peretz. Yiddish writers continued their efforts to modernize Jewish life, but they also fought hard against anti-Semitism and for equal rights for Jews. Jewish nationalism mounted in Eastern Europe. The poet Chaim Nachman Bialik (1873–1934) created a powerful modern idiom in Hebrew but it was through Yiddish, the language of the *shtetl*, that he and others found their greatest audience. Their goal was to be accessible to the everyday reader. Yes, they wanted to appear in the best literary journals, but they did not cut and trim their work to suit the limited, cultivated audience. They also sought publication in the mass-circulation press.

By the 1890s Yiddish literature had found new soil to grow in. The Jewish masses were moving into the cities and entering the working class. They joined trade unions, went on strike, plunged into socialism, Zionism, Yiddishism, reached out for education and culture. Writers responded to the awakening, and through Yiddish fiction and poetry helped plant new ideas in their readers' minds. Eliakum Zunser (1836–1913) was among the earliest. A Vilna writer, his satires and poems were read and recited, sung and chanted everywhere in the Pale.

Mendele Mocher Sforim (pen name of Sholem Jacob Abramowitz, 1836–1917) earned his living as principal of a Jewish school in Odessa. He began his literary career in Hebrew but soon asked himself what good was this work if his writings were of no use to his people. He turned to Yiddish to depict the tragicomic characters of the Pale, writing bitter novels which cried out to the Jews to struggle for a better life.

One of his great followers was Solomon Rabinowitz (1859–1916), who wrote as Sholem Aleichem. He began in Hebrew too but at twenty-four published the first of those Yiddish stories which would win him universal recognition as the voice of the Jewish people. He was at once a popular entertainer and a major artist.

Another founding father of Jewish literature was Isaac Leib Peretz (1852–1915). He began publishing in Yiddish while still a teenager, practiced law, and then served as a functionary in the Warsaw Jewish Civic Center. He developed a pithy idiomatic Yiddish that drew upon folk tales to illuminate the Jewish renaissance. Around him flourished Warsaw's Jewish literary life, and to him many young writers came for guidance.

Thus what is called *Yiddishkeit* blossomed. The word means Yiddishness, a Jewish culture linked to the Yiddish language. There was still resistance to its use. The early Jewish socialists, hostile to both Judaism and Jewish culture, rejected Yiddish. Even the Bund, the pioneer Jewish socialist movement in Eastern Europe, at first used Yiddish reluctantly, out of necessity, as the only way to reach the working class. Later the Bundists realized the enormous value of sustaining Jewish culture while building an economic and political movement. And Yiddish became the beloved tongue, the core of their strength. The Zionists, too, in their infant years despised Yiddish and folk culture because they were part of the millennia of exile. It took a while to overcome this negation of everything creative which had emerged in the Diaspora. Eventually all came to find in the culture of *Yiddishkeit* the foundation they could build on.

A major dilemma is the very ground of the existence of *Yiddishkeit*, as Irving Howe and Eliezer Greenberg point out.

> *For insofar as the Yiddish writers continued in the path of their own tradition, they could not open themselves sufficiently to the surrounding cultures of Europe and America, nor engage themselves sufficiently with the styles and values of modernity to which they now and again aspired. Yet insofar as they accepted the secular cultures of their time, they risked the loss of historical identity, a rupture with that sacred past which could still stir the skeptics quite as much as the believers. . . . It* [Yiddishkeit] *had always to accept the burden of being at home neither entirely with its past nor entirely with the surrounding nations. Out of its marginality it made a premise for humaneness and out of its strivings to elevate Yiddish into a literary language, an experience of intellectual beauty.*

The energy of *Yiddishkeit* generated by Eastern Europe's Jews was carried by the immigrants to America. Of the founding masters, only Sholem Aleichem reached New

York, and very late in life. But many younger Yiddish
writers came over with the mass migration. The first group,
who arrived in the last two decades of the nineteenth
century, were called the "sweatshop poets." Their poems
grew out of the experiences they shared with the immigrant
workers.

The major influence on the early immigrant poets was
Morris Winchevsky (1856–1932). He learned about socialism in Russia and Germany, and by twenty-one had
published satires and poems in both Hebrew and Yiddish.
Expelled from Germany as a revolutionary, he moved to
London, where he spent fifteen years as an editor and
writer in the Jewish labor movement. In the 1880s he
published the first socialist pamphlets to appear in Yiddish.
But he was a poet above all, writing fresh Yiddish lyrics
about working-class life which won wide readership on both
sides of the Atlantic.

When he moved to New York in 1894 he was welcomed
as the *zeide* (grandfather) of the Jewish socialist movement. He was, says Melech Epstein, "practically the sole
socialist veteran whose internationalism did not contradict
his Jewishness." In his role as the great awakener he
reached and moved the younger poets.

One of these was David Edelstadt (1866–92), a childhood witness of the Kiev pogrom of 1881. At sixteen he
fled Russia for America and for three long years made
buttonholes in a Cincinnati garment factory. He began
writing passionate protest poems in the Yiddish he learned
from his shopmates, then moved to New York to edit *Die
Freie Arbeiter Stimme*. Stricken with tuberculosis, the
sweatshop disease, he died at twenty-six. Like Winchevsky's poems, Edelstadt's were set to music and as hymns

and marching songs were sung by Jewish workers everywhere. The revolutionary lyricist Joseph Bovshover (1872–1915) burned out too by the same age, though he lived on much longer. He had a Jewish schooling in Russia and knew Yiddish well when he arrived in New York in 1891. The next year, upon the death of Edelstadt, he wrote an elegy which brought his gift to public attention. Emotionally unstable, he drifted about, living on odd jobs and aid from friends or family. His translation into Yiddish of *The Merchant of Venice* and his lyrics brought him acclaim. But by the age of twenty-six he had sunk into a deep depression and he lived out the rest of his years in a mental institution.

It was Morris Rosenfeld (1862–1923) who received the greatest attention from the non-Jewish world. He was born into a family of fishermen in Poland and given a Jewish education in Warsaw. At eighteen he married, apprenticed briefly in Holland as a diamond cutter, then moved to London, where he worked in sweatshops for three years, writing his poems at night and circulating them among the workers. Poor and sick, he migrated to America in 1886, hearing that the tailors had won a strike which shortened their hours. But in New York it was again the drudgery of fifteen-hour days in the sweatshops, living on stale bread to save the pennies for bringing his wife and children over.

Somehow he managed to study the poetry of great writers, especially Heine, and to attempt the first Yiddish lyrics to abide by the rules of prosody. His best work boiled up out of his hatred for the sweatshop. The poems indicted the system which encouraged the brutal exploitation of man by man. His personal suffering and his anger were powerfully expressed in a simple and idiomatic Yiddish.

His was the true voice of the worker. When the first volume of his Yiddish verse appeared, it was highly praised by Professor Leo Wiener of Harvard in *The Nation*. Wiener then edited a prose translation of the poems under the title *Songs of the Ghetto*. Other critics joined in hailing Rosenfeld as an authentic and important poet. Yiddish was coming into its own as a respectable literary medium.

Pleased by this response, wealthy German-American Jews tried to rescue Rosenfeld from the sweatshop by setting him up in a candy-store business. He detested that too and quit to make his living in journalism and on public platforms, reading his poems. His later verse dropped in quality. He was overpraised simply because he was among the first Yiddish poets; he had the painful experience of seeing his reputation grow dimmer and dimmer. But his satiric journalism was always pointed and pungent. His prose, said Joseph Opatoshu, "is as significant as his poetry; perhaps even more so for the historian seeking to familiarize himself with the Jewish life of that period."

It was the immigrants arriving after the failure of the 1905 Revolution in Russia who birthed a new kind of Yiddish writing. They never considered going back to the old country. They struck new roots here which flowered in a new literature. Called "Die Yunge" (The Young), this group rejected the social preaching of the sweatshop poets in favor of an artistic self-sufficiency. They spurned the traditional sentimentalism of the older writers and would not accept the notion that Yiddish was only a tool destined for the junk heap. Another group soon formed, called the Introspectivists. They worked toward modernism and free verse. Neither group was a school or cult, but rather a force protesting mediocrity and struggling for a Yiddish literature whose justification would no longer be as a means of enlightenment but as an artistic end in itself.

Joseph Opatoshu (1886–1954), a Polish Jew who came to New York in 1907 at the age of twenty-one, saw America as a new center of the Diaspora. He cut leather soles in a shoe factory, sewed shirts in a sweatshop, delivered newspapers, and mastered civil engineering. His short stories and novels began to appear in 1910, earning him a major place in Yiddish literature. He had this to say about the Yiddish writers of that time:

> *Every people creates spiritual resources; folk resources are created haphazardly. Out of these folk resources artists who can see and listen, with alert senses, create order. Mendele was the greatest among these artists. But there are artists who do not depend upon the resources of the folk. These are insufficient for them. Such artists seek to fathom the power that creates a people, they want to discover if that power is also within them as artists. I know the universe to which Mendele and Rosenfeld belong. Peretz's universe, however, as it seeks to discover and liberate itself, is not that easy to grasp. This spirit which strives to liberate itself was always present among Jews; whether in Judah Halevi or Peretz, poets of genius sought and found their justification in Jewish life. The American Yiddish writers of whom I am speaking—Yehoash, Liessin, Pinski, Halpern, Rolnik, Mani Leib, I. J. Schwartz, Leivick, Boraisho, Leyeles, Glatstein, Siegel—all sought and found those depths of Judah Halevi and Peretz. . . . Yiddish literature in America is still a multibranched tree that sheds its withered leaves and grows new ones, fresh ones.*

18 | To Shake the World

In her eightieth year Pauline Newman could still remember what it was like to help bring the labor movement to birth on the Lower East Side. She was barely eight when she got her first job in a garment shop. She had arrived from a Lithuanian *shtetl* in 1901, settling in New York with her family. That same year she went to work at the Triangle Shirtwaist Company.

> *We were kids. When the operator was finished with the machine, we had scissors to cut off the threads that were left over when they pulled out the shirtwaists. We worked from 7:30 in the morning until 8 or 9 at night. No overtime, no supper money. Seven days, but on Sunday you might work only until noon or 2, and that was a half day. There were signs that warned, "If you don't come in Sunday, don't come in Monday."*
>
> *The two people who ran Triangle were damnable, the worst of the lot, and I worked for a number of bosses. But these wouldn't even talk to you. You were not allowed to sing. On Saturday they handed you an envelope*

with $1.50, your salary for the week. By the end of eight years there, in 1909, I had worked up to $6. I was promoted to cut threads from the embroidery that had been inserted into the shirtwaist.

Get another job somewhere else? But the alternatives weren't any better. Pay and working conditions were bad throughout the industry. In the early 1880s the Knights of Labor had tried to help the women's garment workers to organize. With no lasting success, for labor had no rights in law and the public was indifferent. The long-suffering Jewish workers would flare up in despair every once in a while, strike for a raise in the busy season, get a few pennies and return to work, only to see their wages slashed in the slack season. "Seasonal union!" snorted the professional organizers; they thought these immigrants were hopeless union material. They did not understand that the strike was often the workers' only way to protest against a mass society trying to transform them into zeros. They were the nobodies, demanding recognition from the somebodies.

In 1887 there were thirty such futile strikes in New York, and many more elsewhere. The next year a few socialists decided it was time to educate the Jews in trade unionism. Men like Abraham Cahan and Morris Hillquit, intellectual radicals, knew you couldn't leave change to spontaneity. They helped form the United Hebrew Trades in New York. All they could find alive were two infant Jewish unions—the typesetters and the chorus singers—with a grand total of forty members. The UHT's first forays were made among the Jewish actors, the knee-pants makers, and the bakery workers.

Among the Eastern European Jews arriving in those

decades were revolutionaries with creeds and programs they were sure would shake the world, America included. Some were orthodox socialists, followers of Marx and Engels; some were violent anarcho-syndicalists of the Bakunin school; some were believers in Kropotkin's peaceful, philosophical anarchism. And while many were well educated, others were half baked. Most of the radical intellectuals were young, passionate, and devoted to "uplifting the masses." They were the levers needed for that gigantic task.

The trouble was, there were so many ideas about how to do it. No movement can be free of theories. It takes ideas to give a movement meaning and direction. But the labor and radical movements of the late nineteenth and the early twentieth century were torn by bitter factional feuds and contradictory dogmas. Some people believed in one big union for all workers; they were against political action and distrusted all government. Then there were the anarcho-syndicalist ideas which animated both the Knights of Labor (founded in 1869) and then the Industrial Workers of the World, founded a generation later. The American Federation of Labor, started by the Jewish cigar maker Samuel Gompers in 1886, believed in "pure and simple" unionism. But as industry grew bigger and bigger and monopolies took control of huge sections of the country's economy, labor had to move from purely economic action to political action if it was to survive. The Knights and the IWW failed to adjust to the changing America, and died.

When it was clear the AFL was winning out over the Knights, the socialists among the garment workers began to orient themselves toward its more effective unionism. During the early 1890s the New York cloak makers struck

A union local—the Children's Jacket Makers Union of the United Garment Workers—is housed in a row of East Side tenements next door to a dressmaker

against the sweatshops but this time sought help from the United Hebrew Trades. Joseph Barondess was sent in to lead the union to victory. In Chicago, Boston, Baltimore, Philadelphia, the same shift from seasonal to permanent labor unions took place. The New York cloak makers struck again, this time welcoming support from the AFL, and won new gains. The fledgling union tried to extend itself nationwide in the trade but collapsed under factional pressures. Rival unions tossed by political storms appeared and disappeared. Where most of the workers were women and girls, the infant unions died fast, chiefly because the top organizers were men grossly indifferent to the needs of women. But everywhere the idea of unionism caught fire and many branches of the garment trade began to organize.

By the turn of the century the Socialist Party had formed out of earlier radical groups, under the leadership of Eugene V. Debs and Victor Berger, and the *Jewish Daily Forward* was launched with Cahan at the helm. Both forces opposed dual unions and helped organize the garment workers. By now almost a third of the industry's labor force was made up of women and girls. They worked in the dress, shirtwaist, and white-goods branches. "We didn't know much about trade unions or organization," Pauline Newman recalls, "but we had the spirit and fortitude. We believed that things had to get better." Like it or not, the labor chiefs realized they had to organize the women if the unions were to survive.

A national union was badly needed for an industry which now ranked among the major makers of consumer goods. By 1900 there were over 80,000 workers employed in some 2,700 shops. That June delegates from several cities and locals met in New York to form an industrial union of all

crafts in the women's garment trades. They named it the
International Ladies' Garment Workers' Union. A few
weeks later the AFL issued a charter to the new ILGWU.
It grew fast, climbing to 51 locals with 10,000 members by
1903. Half the members worked outside New York and a
third were women. For several years a long depression and
raids by the IWW set the union back badly. But as the
depression began to lift in 1909, the union made a come-
back. "The girls took the lead," said Pauline Newman. "In
those days the men didn't believe that women would stick
to a union. Our union was one of the first not to differen-
tiate between men and women." About 80 percent of the
shirtwaist makers were women, most of them between sixteen and twenty-five. Almost half of them arrived not long
ago from Eastern Europe, radicalized by the Bund and the
Russian revolutionary movement. Although the tenement
sweatshops had almost disappeared, merciless exploitation
continued in the new factory lofts. As business improved,
the workers began to rebel openly against conditions and
their leaders started talking up a general strike to build the
union and win recognition from the manufacturers.

But the International was cold to such a daring proposal.
The women found encouragement only from the Women's
Trade Union League. The League was a new part of the
progressive movement, sponsored by middle-class and professional women, among them the muckraking journalist
Ida Tarbell and the settlement-house leader Lillian Wald.
The only working-class woman among them was Rose
Schneiderman. They were in the feminist stream, concerned to help women win equal rights by working for
labor legislation and union organization. Taking heart from
the ardent support of the League, the shirtwaist makers
tested their strength with shop disputes and walkouts.

On November 22 they held a mass meeting at Cooper Union. For two hours the platform speakers droned on, until suddenly a teenager asked for the floor. It was Clara Lemlich, a fiery unionist who had been beaten by cops on the picket lines. She exploded into Yiddish:

I am a working girl, one of those who are on strike against intolerable conditions. I am tired of listening to speakers who talk in general terms. What we are here for is to decide whether we shall or shall not strike. I offer a resolution that a general strike shall be declared— NOW!

Instantly the audience rose to its feet, shouting, waving arms and hats and handkerchiefs. For five minutes the uproar continued until the chairman, B. Feigenbaum, asked if anyone seconded Clara's motion. Again the big audience leaped up, everyone yelling, "Second!" Carried away, the chairman summoned up the power of old religious ritual. "Do you mean faith? Will you take the old Jewish oath?" he asked. And up came two thousand hands as the two thousand voices chanted in Yiddish, "If I turn traitor to the cause I now pledge, may my right hand wither from this arm I now raise!"

And the historic Uprising of the Twenty Thousand, as it has come to be known, began. Five hundred shops closed down as the shirtmakers and dressmakers, most of them young women, took to the picket line. The Triangle Shirtwaist factory, where Pauline Newman worked, was one of them. Two months before, a hundred of its workers had gone to a secret meeting to organize a union, but the names leaked out and many workers were fired. The United Hebrew Trades, the Socialist Party, the Women's Trade

Union League, all rallied their members to help the strikers. There was frequent fighting on the picket lines between the workers and goons hired to break the strike. The police and the judges took the side of the employers and flooded the courts and the cells with arrested picketers. Sentencing one striker, a judge said, "You are on strike against God and nature, whose firm law is that man shall earn his bread in the sweat of his brow. You are on strike against God!" But the girls did not frighten. Hundreds bloomed overnight as leaders, speakers, organizers. They raced from hall to hall to address strikers, they battled cops and scabs on the streets, they raised money for relief, they sought support before community groups, they went round the clock without food or sleep. Arrested almost daily, they would be bailed out and hurry back to the battle. Only fourteen, Pauline Newman was sent upstate by the union to raise money for the strikers. It was her first trip out of New York, but she came home from Buffalo with $250 from unionists there.

The newspapers and the public were swept into strike support by the electric energy, the courage and devotion of these young women. Appalled by the exposure of shop conditions, thousands jammed a huge mass meeting the union held in the Hippodrome. The strike soon spread to Philadelphia. But finally, on February 15, it came to an official end. The results, though marking an important advance, were scattered. Many of the smaller shops had settled earlier, thereby weakening the effort to win a general settlement. The big firms had managed to hold out and in the end gave no recognition to the union. But in the older branches of the industry, where men predominated on the job, the spark had been ignited. Now the cloak makers, too,

Headquarters of the Women's Trade Union League during the
Uprising of the Twenty Thousand

were calling for a general strike. The union leaders had learned the lesson that women counted, and could be counted on. And valuable ties between the middle-class reform movement and labor had been made. It was an alliance that would grow over the next decades into a strong influence on political life.

Five months later the New York cloak makers voted overwhelmingly for a general strike. The strike had been prepared systematically and brought out 60,000 workers. It was "a gigantic uprising of a whole people against their oppressors." The demands made included not only improvements in wages, hours, and working conditions but union recognition and a closed shop. More than three hundred of the smaller shops settled soon, but the employers refused to begin bargaining unless the closed-shop demand was dropped in advance. Jewish leaders were angered by their inhuman stubbornness and pressured them to negotiate before they ruined the good name of the Jewish community. Movement began when a board of arbitration, made up of such powerful Jewish leaders as Louis Marshall, Jacob Schiff, and Louis D. Brandeis, stepped in. Brandeis (who would later serve on the Supreme Court) was a distinguished lawyer from Boston who had counseled business and labor in the past. Together with Samuel Gompers he was able to get both sides to agree in September on a settlement called the Protocol of Peace.

The agreement set better standards for wages, hours, and working conditions, and gave the union official recognition. But in place of the closed shop, a Brandeis formula for the "preferential shop" was accepted. It meant that if competing job applicants were otherwise equal, the union man would get preference. It was a favorable end for labor to the nine-week "Great Revolt of 1910" and the greatest victory New York workers had yet won. For in establishing the principle of collective bargaining it helped the whole labor movement in its struggle for justice.

If anything else was needed to make labor and the public alike realize how important unions were, the shock was provided seven months later. It began at 4:45 on the afternoon on March 25, 1911. The 850 employees in the city's biggest shirtwaist factory, Triangle, had one hour to go before quitting time. Most of them were young girls. (Pauline Newman was not among them; she had gone to work for the union after the strike.) The company occupied the seventh, eighth, and ninth floors of a ten-story building at Washington Place and Greene Street, close by Washington Square. A man going to the toilet lit a cigarette on the way and dropped his match to the floor. The tiny flame touched scraps from the cutting table and a fire blazed up. The cutters and designers working at the tables ran into the hallway and yanked the fire hose from its stand. They raced back to the flames, but the hose, rotted at the folds, broke into pieces. The fire reached highly inflammable cleaning fluids and in seconds huge tongues of flame were darting out of the windows.

Some of the panic-stricken girls rushed for the rear exit, forgetting the bosses locked it every afternoon to force the workers to stand inspection for pilferage at the front door as they left work. The heavy iron door would not give way to pounding fists and battering bodies. Some workers thought of the fire escape and ran for it. It was a lone ladder going down to a narrow rear court and up to the roof. Only one small door gave access to it. The girls struggled to get through, breathing fire and choking on smoke. About seventy made it to the roof or the street that way. Many others reached the elevators, and were rushed to

A strike demonstration in Union Square

safety by the elevator men, who risked the ascent and descent a score of times until, twenty minutes later, fire streaming into the shaft and licking at the cables made them stop.

Ten minutes after the first alarm had been given, the firemen reached the building. Their ladders climbed only to the sixth floor and their hoses jetted only to the seventh. They spread nets on the street below; above, at the blazing windows, women and men could be seen leaning far out, mouths screaming wide.

Morris Rosenfeld, the sweatshop poet, told *Forward* readers what happened, building his account from eyewitness reports.

> One girl after another fell, like shot birds, from above, from the burning floors. The men held out a longer time, enveloped in flames. And when they could hold out no longer, they jumped, too.
>
> Below, horrified and weeping, stood thousands of workers from the surrounding factories. They watched moving, terrible, unforgettable scenes. At one window on the eighth floor appeared a young man with a girl. He was holding her tightly by the hand. Behind them the red flames could be seen. The young man lovingly wrapped his arms around the girl and held her to him a moment, kissed her, and then let her go. She leaped, and fell to the sidewalk with great impact. A moment later he leaped after her, and his body landed next to hers. Both were dead. . . .
>
> It took a whole hour before the firemen could enter the burning building, and by then it was all over. The sidewalks were full of dead and wounded, and no one could be seen at the windows any longer. The poor girls

Victims of the fire that devastated the Triangle Shirtwaist factory in 1911 are placed in coffins on the sidewalk, waiting to be taken to the morgue. The disaster killed 146, most of them young women

who had remained inside the building lay all about burnt or smothered to death by fire and smoke. The ambulances and patrol wagons that arrived were not sufficient for the job. Grocers, butchers, and peddlers contributed their wagons and pushcarts. Dozens of stores were transformed into hospitals or morgues.

The catapult force of the long plunges made the nets useless. The bodies tore the nets from the firemen's grasp or ripped right through the cords to the pavement. By 8 P.M. the supply of coffins had given out and the morgue sent back many already used once. Now bodies were being taken out of the building at the rate of one per minute and sometimes four or six coffins were loaded together on the waiting wagons. The crews of police and morgue attendants were so overcome by the appalling task they had to be replaced three times before the work was done.

On April 7 a mass funeral took place in the rain. Fifty thousand people marched silently through the Lower East Side in remembrance of the dead. But more than the lost lives were remembered. The conditions immigrants were forced to work under had been glaringly illuminated by the flames. The mourning was mixed with rage. Harris and Blanck, the Triangle partners, were tried for manslaughter, and acquitted. Still, the social meaning of the disaster was not lost. Humane middle- and upper-class Americans already concerned with urban reform now saw that infinitely more had to be done for justice and equality. Not "the inscrutable decrees of Divine Providence," but the greed of unscrupulous men accounted for these preventable disasters.

A Factory Investigating Commission was appointed by New York State. For three years it examined industrial working conditions, heard testimony on proposals to deal with them, and prepared reports for the legislature to consider. The lawmakers overhauled the state's industrial code with thirty-five new measures.

Out of the Triangle tragedy came a revolution in laws for protection of the workers in factories—fire prevention, factory inspection, liability insurance, workmen's compensation. The garment workers' own organization, the ILGWU, became a spearhead of reform and ultimately one of the leading labor unions in America. The trades the Jewish immigrants had taken to were one after another unionized: the Cap Makers in 1901, the Fur Workers in 1904, the Amalgamated Clothing Workers in 1914. By 1918 over a quarter of a million Jewish workers were affiliated through their unions with the United Hebrew Trades.

Despite the hopes of the Protocol of Peace, the unions enjoyed no lasting security. In the cities beyond the Hudson the employers stuck to the open shop. It took a long time for the unions to defeat the hire-and-fire policy. Not until the New Deal of the 1930s did collective bargaining become a legally enforced right. One of the labor leaders who helped bring about that enormous change was Sidney Hillman.

Born in an Eastern European village in 1887, Hillman had gone to the famous yeshiva of Slobodka. Turning radical, he left to join the Bund. He was arrested in the 1905 revolutionary year and served six months in prison. In 1907 he became one of the many refugees from the Russian Revolution and settled in Chicago. From cutter's apprentice in a men's clothing factory he rose through labor's ranks to president of the new Amalgamated Clothing Workers—the equivalent in the men's garment industry of the ILGWU.

Hillman came to see the strike as a desperate weapon in jungle warfare. While the young radical Jews and Italians in the shops talked class warfare, his pragmatic mind sought ways to convince employers that acceptance of the union was to their advantage as well as the workers'. Like other Jewish labor leaders, he turned his energy toward the democratization of industry. He stimulated joint union-management activities. He was the first garment union leader to encourage technological progress in production, and to set up a research department to plan for scientific management. His union led the way in providing unemployment benefits, establishing the only successful labor bank, and building low-cost cooperative housing.

It was the Jewish socialists who deserve credit for organizing the Jewish immigrant workers. No one else was capable of carrying out that task, says C. Belzalel Sherman.

Their great achievement was that they transformed these degraded Jewish immigrants into a social force which not only altered the course of Jewish history in the United States but left its mark on the country's entire labor movement. The remarkable thing was that these beaten-down laborers, who worked under such abominable conditions, who were not part of a tradition of independent trade union action, who were worlds away from a proletarian psychology, and who were, perhaps in their majority, Orthodox in religion, founded their first trade unions as socialist organizations. The socialist ideology of the leaders found a warm response in the sense of social justice that lived in the soul of the ordinary Jew—a sense that derived from a combination of the prophetic vision and his unjust treatment at the hands of the non-Jewish world.

In 1893 Eliakum Zunser, the Vilna folk poet, wrote this song about the America he discovered in his last years.

In di enge gasn, vu di mase
    shteyt gedicht,
Fil orime, finstere, der unglik
    ligt oyfn gezicht;

Shteyen fun fri biz baynacht,

De lipn ferbrent un fershmacht.
Der iz mafkir zayn kind far a
    sent,
Dem varft men fun voynung far
    rent,
Fil grine mit shvern gemit,

Faln fun hunger in *strit,*
Fil dalis mit krankhayt banand,
Alts in dem goldenem land.

Dem arbeter's lebn shvimt do
    avek
In a taych fun zayn eygenem
    shveys;
Horevet in *bizi* un hungert in
    slek,
Un iz shtendig in shrek mit zayn
    pleys.
. . . Der proletar hot do a vert,

Punkt vi in *stritkars* di ferd,
Loyft, loyft, bizvaneh er
    falt. . . .

In the narrow streets, where the
    mass stands compressed,
There are many poor and
    miserable, unhappiness is on
    every face.
They stand from morning till
    night,
Their lips parched and burned.
One sacrifices his child for a
    cent,
Another is thrown from his
    dwelling for not paying rent,
Many immigrants in depressed
    mood,
Fall from hunger on the street,
Much poverty and sickness, too,
Are all found in this golden land.

The worker's life flows away here

In a river of his own sweat;

He toils during the busy season
    and starves in the slack
And is always in fear of losing his
    job.
The proletarian has as much
    worth here
As the horses pulling the
    streetcars,
Running, running, until he
    falls. . . .

19 | The Door Closes

With the coming of World War I in 1914 there was a vast upheaval in Jewish life. The major battlegrounds of the Eastern Front were the homelands of the Jews. Hunger, disease, and massacre became the common fate. In 1917, Messianic hopes were rekindled when Czarism was overthrown, the Russian Jews emancipated, and the Balfour Declaration issued by Britain favoring the establishment in Palestine of a national homeland for the Jewish people.

The immigrant Jews in America saw in these grand events salvation for their kindred. But it did not come about. Eastern Europe fell into bloody chaos, with civil war drowning Jewish hopes in waves of pogroms. And here at home, a nativist outburst against aliens was triggered by the trauma of the war. When President Woodrow Wilson preached "a crusade to save the world for democracy," it had the paradoxical effect of causing repression at home. Wilson himself said, "Once lead this people into war and they'll forget that there was ever such a thing as tolerance." As American troops joined the battle, a reign of terror was launched against those who opposed the war on pacifist or radical grounds or because of ethnic sympathies. Dissenters were whipped, tarred and feathered, and a few even lynched. Volunteer informers made antiwar talk dangerous and new Espionage and Sedition laws powered the crusade for conformity. Over 1,500 radicals were arrested, the IWW was suppressed, and many of the left-wing and ethnic newspapers were muzzled.

The nativists were especially rabid against Jews and Catholics and Americans of German origin. Immigrants hoping to become Americans were pressed even harder than before to slough off every trace of Old World custom and culture. Many states adopted laws banning the use of foreign languages in school instruction.

Two years later one of the unhappiest episodes in nativist hysteria erupted. Attorney General A. Mitchell Palmer, an ambitious Democrat seeking the Presidency, ordered federal agents to conduct a mass roundup of "Reds." In one night his men raided thirty-three cities and netted over 4,000 "suspected" radicals, most of them immigrants. The victims were held for days, weeks, months, to be deported "back to where they came from" or jailed for twenty-year sentences. In that Red Scare period intense suffering was inflicted upon thousands of people who, radical or not, had a right to their beliefs. The weak and fragmented radical movement was no threat to anyone. Yet the federal government brushed aside the Bill of Rights to carry out ruthless suppression.

Dislike for the Jew, as in any time of social crisis, had begun to rise with the onset of the war. Everything "foreign" and "radical" was under suspicion. Politicians like Palmer, intent on advancing their political careers, saw that fending off these internal devils promised special rewards.

By riding popular fears they might reach high office. Tom Watson, a Southern populist who had long attacked the blacks, turned against the Catholics, and then began baiting the Jews on the platform and in the press. In 1915, Leo Frank, a young Jew from the North, was accused of murdering a girl in the Atlanta factory where he worked, and convicted on the flimsiest evidence. Watson ranted that the way to get rid of Jewish interference in Georgia was to execute Frank. A brave governor commuted Frank's death sentence. Watson's inflamed followers abducted Frank from jail and lynched him.

It was during these years that many books were written voicing fears about the new immigration. One of the most influential was Madison Grant's *The Passing of the Great Race* (1916). Grant, anthropologist at the American Museum of Natural History, repeated the supposed proofs of Jewish inferiority which the British anti-Semite Houston Stewart Chamberlain was promoting. Both argued that human inequality was a fact, and that if inferior peoples (this "wretched, submerged, human-flotsam of the Polish ghettos") were not segregated, the superior people (Nordics) would be in danger. (Hitler became one of Chamberlain's passionate disciples.) As popular a book was Lothrop Stoddard's *The Rising Tide of Color* (1920).

But it was not only from conservatives that racist appeals came. Historians, sociologists, and economists who were progressive by the standards of the day wrote such books too. The scholars John R. Commons, Edward A. Ross, and Henry Pratt Fairchild all held that the superiority of democracy was due to the superiority of Anglo-Saxons. They looked upon the Southern and Eastern European immigrants as ignorant, filthy, coarse breeds, whose mixture with

the old American stocks would mean national degenera-
tion. The rising sentiment against the blacks is recorded in
the many race riots and lynchings, North and South, which
bloody the calendar of that generation. As for the Jew, "the
time has come," said the leader of the St. Petersburg,
Florida, Chamber of Commerce, "to make this a hundred
percent American and gentile city as free from foreigners as
from slums."

In 1916, when President Wilson nominated Brandeis of
Boston for the Supreme Court, a bitter struggle broke out
in the Senate and the country over his confirmation. A
petition signed by over fifty prominent Massachusetts men,
headed by President Lowell of Harvard and studded with
the "best" family names, protested that Brandeis was not
fit for the Bench. But everyone knew the underlying reason
was that the nominee was a Jew. Another protest signed by
seven men who had held the presidency of the American
Bar Association struck the same blow against Brandeis. The
anti-Semitic campaign made the stereotyped accusations
that Brandeis was a trickster and always had a mercenary
motive for his actions. Wilson was nominating him only as
"bait for the Hebrew vote" in the next election. A number
of wealthy and conservative Jews suggested quietly that
Wilson withdraw the nomination because they feared the
uproar it was causing would upset their plans for gaining
status gradually and peacefully. The counsel of the timid
was ignored; Brandeis won (by a very close margin) and
became one of the most distinguished jurists in the Court's
history.

The Russian Revolution of 1917 provided another occasion for anti-Semitic propaganda. It was widely charged
that the Jews had plotted the Communist take-over of

power and now controlled it. The accusation fed neatly into the notorious *Protocols of the Elders of Zion*, an anti-Semitic concoction of a Jewish plot to rule the world. Henry Ford, the auto magnate, spent millions on his weekly newspaper, the *Dearborn Independent*, reprinting the *Protocols* and adding "evidence" of how the plot was going in the United States.

In the 1920s the Ku Klux Klan, a secret society founded in the South after the Civil War to persecute the emancipated blacks, was revived as the bulwark of 100 percent Americanism. Now it declared itself the foe not only of blacks but of Catholics and Jews as well. The KKK's *Fiery Cross* warned that "the Jews dominated the economic life of the nation while the Catholics are determined to dominate the political and religious life." Its appeal to racism rallied over five million members, chiefly in the small towns and rural regions of the South and Midwest.

Those millions were susceptible to racist ideas because, says the historian George E. Mowry:

> *The Klan represented a deeply troubled group of Americans, recruited mainly from the countryside, conscious of their growing inferiority, and deeply sensitive to the destruction of their traditional values by the new mass-producing, mass-consuming culture of the burgeoning cities. . . . They readily accepted the technology and the financial and selling techniques upon which the new mass culture rested, but they assailed its social results. Needing a villain, they turned to the convenient Catholic, Negro, and Jew, who together had probably far less to do with the destruction of the ancient rural heritage than their fellow Protestant Ameri-*

*cans caught up with the glittering material promises of
the great boom.*

These fellow Protestant Americans included a select
group in the Northeast, remote from the "hicks and rubes
and drivers of second-hand Fords," which is how Imperial
Wizard Hiram Evans described his KKK followers. But the
Boston Brahmins looked upon the new immigrants in
much the same way. To Senator Henry Cabot Lodge, the
powerful Republican, these "inferior" people were invaders
as dangerous to America as the Goths and Vandals who
trampled over Rome. He pushed a bill in Congress to
require all European immigrants to prove their ability to
read and write for admission. It was the best legal device to
keep out undesirables.

Nathaniel Shaler, dean of Harvard's Graduate School of
Science, was another spokesman from polite and educated
circles who gave respectability to the notion that Southern
and Eastern Europeans were radically inferior. Less "scientific" but equally poisonous were the views of the historian
Henry Adams, friend of Lodge, who recoiled in horror
when he encountered a "furtive Jacob or Ysaac still reeking
of the Ghetto, snarling a weird Yiddish." "The Jew," he
wrote, "makes me creep."

The old established families of Boston and New York
resented the incursion of prosperous Jews into their society.
Nearly all of them were anti-Semitic. The novelist Henry
James, returning home for a visit in 1904, after a long
sojourn abroad, was repelled by the new America. But
disgusted especially by the "swarming" Jews he saw on a
tour of the Lower East Side. They reminded him of "small,
strange animals . . . snakes or worms. . . ." It was the

same dehumanized response as Hitler's view of the Jews as bacilli or vermin. Neither could see a Jew as an individual, only as a stereotype.

What joined Boston Brahmin, university professor, and KKK'er in a common belief? They were frightened by the tumultuous growth of industry and cities. They blamed the newcomers for depressing wages, lowering living standards, creating slums, committing crime, spreading disease. "There emerged a sense," says the historian John J. Appel, "that the American people must define what was American, what alien. Many older Americans were uneasy, even fearful over what appeared to be the breakdown of ethnic homogeneity and the loss of old values. . . . Unlike those liberals who by the 1900s had begun to accept the necessity for regulation but insisted on the continued ability of American society to assimilate the newcomers, those favoring their exclusion on racist and nativist grounds saw themselves as the true defenders of traditional ideals of the United States as the most perfect society on earth, its customs and values fixed, to be protected from alien assault and perversion."

The president of the AFL, too, added his voice to the chorus calling for restriction of immigration. When the U.S. Immigration Commission issued a massive report in 1911, paving the way for racist quota laws, Gompers gave organized labor's official support to it. Most of the American craft unions had long tried to exclude strangers. And now Gompers found himself teamed up with Senator Lodge in seeking to curb the new immigration.

In 1917, after several attempts, Congress passed a bill, over Wilson's veto, which limited immigration through the literacy test Lodge had urged. When immigrants began coming in again after the war, the nativists decided the literacy barrier was not enough. In 1921, Congress passed a temporary law introducing the principle of numerical restriction based upon nationality. It was a stopgap until 1924 when the Johnson-Reed Act slammed the door on mass immigration. It set a ceiling of 150,000 a year. A quota formula was adopted that would remain in effect for forty-one years. The law fixed the quota of each nation at 2 percent of the number of its immigrants here in 1890. After 1929 a permanent ceiling of 150,000 persons a year was set, with quotas based on the 1920 census. With more than two thirds of the Americans in 1920 of Northern European ancestry, the goal was clear: to keep Nordics *über alles*. The much larger numbers of people in Southern and Eastern Europe who desired to immigrate sat on long waiting lists. They could not enter because their small quotas were always filled. (Not until 1965 did Congress end the national origins quotas.) The effect of the 1924 law upon the Jews is one example of the way the new measure worked. In that year, the last year of mass immigration, 50,000 Jews entered the country. In the next, 10,000. The flood of Jewish immigration had been dammed. And the great century of migration was over.

It was in these years that American Jews became the targets of an extended system of exclusion. In the Gilded Age, entrenched wealth had begun to shut Jews out from society. The fashionable resorts and hotels made known they did not welcome Jews as guests. By the end of the century the pattern had spread to the clubs and even the philanthropic organizations of the cities. High society set the tone, and the middle class aped it. Jews began to find they could not move into any neighborhood they wished.

Informal understandings, "gentlemen's agreements," and restrictive covenants in deeds of sale did the job. By 1910, fields of employment were also being closed off to the outsider. Many of the Jews had been concentrated in a relatively few trades or industries. But as some Jews acquired the training or education to enter different callings, they met discrimination. Many companies had a flat policy against hiring any Jews. Employment agencies helped by never referring Jews to openings. The public press carried ads reading "No Jews Need Apply" or "White Protestants Only." The demand for manpower created by World War I lowered the barriers somewhat, but up they went again, and even higher, in the 1920s. By now many of the biggest businesses in the land—even those which were public utilities or required chartering by the state—considered exclusion of the Jews their private privilege.

The professions proved especially attractive to Jews, particularly the first American-born generation. In medicine, law, teaching, engineering, it would seem you need only have the talent and the training to qualify for admission to the free callings. The proper family or financial connections seemed irrelevant. The Jew whose parents had left the *shtetl* only yesterday had just as much right to practice a profession as the son of a Lowell or a Stuyvesant.

But did he? Respectable law and engineering firms would not hire qualified Jews. Colleges and universities between 1870 and 1930 gave professorships to only a handful of Jews. Even the lower rungs of the academic ladder were hard to get hold of. But the worst discrimination occurred in medicine. Membership in medical societies and hospitals, often vital to successful practice, was denied to qualified Jewish physicians. And that restrictive policy soon reached down into medical education itself. As the number of medical schools declined, under pressure to eliminate poor schools and badly trained doctors, Jews were the first to be refused admission.

With all the professions the reasons were pretty much the same. The non-Jews feared competition. They also believed association with Jews would lower their professional and social status. And why risk tainting the profession with these odious outsiders? A major device for exclusion was introduced: the quota system. All medical schools used it to reduce the number of Jewish students.

The same system, sometimes called the *numerus clausus*, was picked up by many private schools and liberal-arts colleges. Jewish students, if not refused altogether, were limited to a tiny fixed quota.

Only gradually did the Jews wake up to what was happening. The immigrants confined to ethnic trades and neighborhoods were unaware of the threat outside. It was the more prosperous Jews who felt it first. Their initial response was defensive. We deserve equal treatment, they argued, because we Jews have been in America since the founding of the colonies, we have served loyally in every American war, we've worked as hard as anyone to build this country.

The discrimination not only persisted, it increased. Argument, no matter how strong, fell on the deaf ear of the prejudiced. Bolder and more practical measures were called for. The B'nai B'rith created its Anti-Defamation League in 1914 to fight against prejudice and discrimination. And the American Jewish Congress and American Jewish Committee joined in. They organized protests, spoke up when public issues such as the immigration quota bill concerned

Jews, used the influence of leading Jews to exert personal pressure at strategic points.

But it was hard to prevail against the growing hostility. How prove, for instance, that the conspiracy charged in the *Protocols* did not exist? Legal action forced Henry Ford to apologize publicly and retract his accusations. But false charges influenced the popular mind through countless pieces of propaganda. The courts ruled that an individual could not be injured by libel against his group. It was almost useless to try to beat out the flames ignited by emotional mass movements.

What the defense organizations could do was to prevent anti-Semitism from turning into law, or influencing government action. The Constitution did protect religious freedom. And luckily, the Klan and other such groups had no practical political program. Their major success in the 1920s was the passage of the immigration quota laws.

Two lessons did emerge from that troubled time. One was that the security of Jews could best be assured by a struggle for the rights of *all* Americans. Jews join in the defense of every minority; the survival of each depends upon the survival of all. The second lesson was that the fate of the Jews is linked to the condition of American democracy. When it is healthy and growing, when it is liberal and progressive, the climate is favorable. Where reaction sets in, Jews are in danger. Serious social and economic problems which go ignored (as soon they would in Germany) prepare the way for demagogues to rise to power, for totalitarianism to crush democracy and wipe out liberty and life. Any society that fears change and suppresses dissent will be hostile to Jews.

Afterword

A book has to end someplace. This one ends with the shutting of the gates upon mass immigration. The immigrant generation I write about paid no attention to an author's limits and insisted upon going on. Some of them, at least those who got here young and just before free entry ended, are still with us. Their lives have been shaped not only by the Lower East Side culture but by the Great Depression of the 1930s, the Holocaust, and the grandchildren's generation of postwar prosperity, Asian wars, Watergate, another economic depression. This book does not follow them into those years. It would be another kind of story altogether.

Bibliography

This is not an exhaustive list of the research materials used in the course of preparing this work. It does not contain references to those valuable sources, the files of contemporary newspapers and periodicals. I should like to mention at least the most important journals and yearbooks whose articles I found especially helpful: *American Hebrew, American Jewish Archives, American Jewish Historical Quarterly, American Jewish Year Book, Commentary, Ethnicity, Jewish Social Studies, Labor History, Publications of the American Jewish Historical Society, Yivo Annual of Jewish Social Science*. And once again I offer special thanks to that indispensable treasure house, the Yivo Institute for Jewish Research, and its librarians, Dina Abramowicz and Bella Weinberg.

The edition of a book given in the following list is the one I used; sometimes it is a later edition than the first. A number of the titles are now available in paperback.

Antin, Mary. *The Promised Land*. Boston: Houghton Mifflin, 1969.

Appel, John J., ed. *The New Immigration*. New York: Pitman, 1971.

Bernheimer, Charles S., ed. *The Russian Jew in the United States*. New York: Ozer, 1971.

Bookbinder, Hyman H. *To Promote the General Welfare: The Story of the Amalgamated Clothing Workers*. New York: Amalgamated Clothing Workers, 1950.

Bremner, Robert H. *From the Depths: The Discovery of Poverty in the United States*. New York: New York University Press, 1956.

Cahan, Abraham. *The Education of Abraham Cahan*. Philadelphia: Jewish Publication Society, 1969.

———. *The Rise of David Levinsky*. New York: Harper Colophon, 1966.

Chotzinoff, Samuel. *A Lost Paradise*. New York: Knopf, 1955.

Chyet, Stanley F., ed. *Lives and Voices*. Philadelphia: Jewish Publication Society, 1972.

Cohen, Morris R. *A Dreamer's Journey*. New York: Free Press, 1949.

Cohen, Samuel H. *Transplanted*. New York, 1937.

Davidson, Gabriel. *Our Jewish Farmers: The Story of the Jewish Agricultural Society*. New York: Fischer, 1943.

Davis, Allen F. *Spearheads for Reform: The Social Settlements and the Progressive Movement, 1890–1914*. New York: Oxford, 1967.

———, and McGree, Mary L. *Eighty Years at Hull-House*. Chicago: Quadrangle, 1969.

Dinnerstein, Leonard. *Anti-Semitism in the U.S.* New York: Holt, 1971.

———, and Jaher, Frederic C., eds. *The Aliens: A History of Ethnic Minorities in America*. New York: Appleton-Century-Crofts, 1970.

Dunne, Thomas. *Ellis Island*. New York: Norton, 1971.

Eisenberg, Azriel, ed. *The Golden Land*. New York: Yoseloff, 1964.

Elbogen, Ismar. *A Century of Jewish Life, 1840–1940*. Philadelphia: Jewish Publication Society, 1944.

Epstein, Melech. *Profiles of Eleven*. Detroit: Wayne State University Press, 1965.

———. *Jewish Labor in the U.S.A.* New York: Ktav, 1969.

Feldstein, Stanley, and Costello, Laurence, eds. *The Ordeal of Assimilation*. New York: Doubleday Anchor, 1974.

Finkelstein, Louis, ed. *The Jews*. 3 vols.; New York: Schocken, 1971.

Fishman, William J. *Jewish Radicals: From Czarist Stetl to London Ghetto*. New York: Pantheon, 1975.

Glazer, Nathan. *American Judaism*. Chicago: University of Chicago Press, 1957.

———, and Moynihan, Daniel Patrick. *Beyond the Melting Pot*. Cambridge: M.I.T. Press, 1963.

Goodman, Henry, ed. *The New Country*. New York: YKUF Publishers, 1961.

Grayzel, Solomon. *A History of the Contemporary Jews: From 1900 to the Present*. New York: Atheneum, 1972.

Greer, Colin. *The Great School Legend*. New York: Basic Books, 1973.

Handlin, Oscar. *The Uprooted*. Boston: Little, Brown, 1956.

———, ed. *Immigration as a Factor in American History*. Englewood Cliffs, N.J.: Prentice-Hall, 1959.

Hapgood, Norman. *The Spirit of the Ghetto*. New York: Schocken, 1966.

Harap, Louis. *The Image of the Jew in American Literature*. Philadelphia: Jewish Publication Society, 1974.

Hartmann, Edward. *The Movement to Americanize the Immigrant*. New York: AMC Press, 1948.

Higham, John. *Strangers in the Land: Patterns of American Nativism, 1860–1925*. New York: Atheneum, 1972.

———. *Send These to Me: Jews and Other Immigrants in Urban America*. New York: Atheneum, 1975.

Hillquit, Morris. *Loose Leaves from a Busy Life*. New York: Macmillan, 1934.

Hindus, Maurice. *Green Worlds*. New York: Doubleday, 1938.

———. *A Traveler in Two Worlds*. New York: Doubleday, 1971.

Hindus, Milton, ed. *The Old East Side*. Philadelphia: Jewish Publication Society, 1971.

Howe, Irving, and Greenberg, Eliezer, eds. *Voices from the Yiddish*. Ann Arbor: University of Michigan Press, 1972.

Jacob, H. E. *World of Emma Lazarus*. New York: Schocken, 1949.

Janowsky, Oscar, ed. *The American Jew*. New York, 1942.

Jones, Maldwyn. *American Immigration*. Chicago: University of Chicago Press, 1960.

Joseph, Samuel. *Jewish Immigration to the United States*. New York: Columbia University Press, 1914.

Juergens, George. *Joseph Pulitzer and the New York World*. Princeton: Princeton University Press, 1966.

Kallen, Horace M. *Culture and Democracy in the United States*. New York: Arno, 1970.

Kaplan, Simon. *Once a Rebel*. New York: Farrar & Rinehart, 1941.

Karp, A. J., ed. *The Jewish Experience in America*. 5 vols.; New York: Ktav, 1969.

Krug, Edwin A. *The Shaping of the American High School: 1880–1920*. Madison: University of Wisconsin Press, 1969.

Lang, Lucy Robbins. *Tomorrow Is Beautiful*. New York: Macmillan, 1948.

Levine, Louis. *The Women's Garment Workers*. New York: B. W. Huebsch.

Lifson, David S. *The Yiddish Theater in America*. New York: Yoseloff, 1965.

Liptzin, Samuel. *Tales of a Tailor*. New York, 1965.

Liptzin, Sol. *Eliakum Zunser*. New York: Behrman, 1950.

Madison, Charles. *Yiddish Literature: Its Scope and Major Writers*. New York: Schocken, 1971.

Metzker, Isaac, ed. *A Bintel Brief*. New York: Ballantine, 1972.

Novak, Michael. *The Rise of the Unmeltable Ethnics.* New York: Macmillan, 1971.

Novotny, Ann. *Strangers at the Door.* New York: Chatham, 1972.

Ravitch, Diane. *The Great School Wars: New York 1805–1973.* New York: Basic Books, 1974.

Reznikoff, Charles. *Family Chronicle.* New York: Universal Books, 1972.

Riis, Jacob A. *How the Other Half Lives.* New York: Scribners, 1890.

———. *Jacob Riis Revisited.* New York: Doubleday Anchor, 1968.

Rischin, Moses. *The Promised City: New York's Jews, 1870–1914.* New York: Harper Torchbook, 1970.

Rosenblum, Gerald. *Immigrant Workers: Their Impact on American Labor Radicalism.* New York: Basic Books, 1973.

Roskolenko, Harry. *The Time That Was Then.* New York: Dial, 1971.

Sachar, Howard M. *The Course of Modern Jewish History.* New York: World, 1958.

Samuel, Maurice. *Little Did I Know.* New York: Knopf, 1963.

Sanders, Ronald. *The Downtown Jews.* New York: Harper, 1969.

Schoener, Allon, ed. *Portal to America: The Lower East Side, 1870–1925.* New York: Holt, 1967.

Schwartz, J. R. *Orchard Street.* New York: Comet Press, 1960.

Scott, Franklin D. *The Peopling of America: Perspectives on Immigration.* Washington: American Historical Association, 1972.

Selzer, Michael, ed. *Kike: Anthology of Anti-Semitism.* New York: World, 1972.

Sherman, C. Belzalel. *The Jew within American Society.* Detroit: Wayne State University Press, 1965.

Sklare, Marshall, ed. *The Jew in American Society*. New York: Behrman, 1974.

Solomon, Barbara M. *Ancestors and Immigrants*. Chicago: University of Chicago Press, 1956.

Soyer, Raphael. *Self-Revealment: A Memoir*. New York: Random House, 1969.

Spargo, John. *The Bitter Cry of the Children*. Chicago: Quadrangle, 1968.

Stein, Leon. *The Triangle Fire*. Philadelphia: Lippincott, 1962.

Sterne, Maurice. *Shadow and Light*. New York: Harcourt, 1965.

Taylor, Philip. *The Distant Magnet: European Emigration to the U.S.A.* New York: Harper Torchbook, 1972.

Teller, Judd L. *Strangers and Natives*. New York: Delta, 1968.

Todd, A. L. *Justice on Trial: The Case of Louis D. Brandeis*. New York: McGraw-Hill, 1964.

Report of the United States Immigration Commission, 61st Cong., 3d sess. 41 vols.; Washington, D.C.: U.S. Government Printing Office, 1911.

Vorspan, Albert. *Giants of Justice*. New York: Union of American Hebrew Congregations, 1960.

Wirth, Louis. *The Ghetto*. Chicago: University of Chicago Press, 1956.

Wischnitzer, Mark. *To Dwell in Freedom: History of Jewish Emigration Since 1800*. Philadelphia: Jewish Publication Society, 1948.

Zorach, William. *Art Is My Life*. New York: World, 1967.

Index